INDIVISIBLE

COMING HOME TO DEEP CONNECTION

CHRISTINE MARIE MASON

For information contact:
www.IndivisibleTheBook.com

ISBN: 978-0-9977277-0-8

First Edition: May, 2016

10 9 8 7 6 5 4 3 2 1

Dedicated to my best teachers:
Jarrett, Samantha, Kyle, Connor, Laurel & Grace

May the world you inherit be more connected, beautiful & whole.
May you, and all beings everywhere, be happy and free.

and to Monika
Jai Ma

ACKNOWLEDGMENTS

This story has been coming for decades, but it was written at this specific moment in time due to the provocation of one person: Steve Beshara, who told me unequivocally to 'stop sending up test balloons' and just start writing a substantive accounting of this path.

Thanks to my long time companion Colin Cook, who encouraged me every step of the way, and added his own brand of goofball wordplay to the writing process. To friends who read portions and gave actionable feedback: Rachael Lamkin, Ali Binazir, Shiva Alcheman, Scott James, Kevin & Susan Stone, Tamsin Smith, Jesse Houk, Joseph Douglas, Fred Burks, Pierre Powell, Jacques Verduin and Sue Mason. Extra acknowledgements to my line editor and dear friend, Jeff Greenwald, and my trusted weekly advisor Alison Hennessee, who kept the process rolling despite all my many distractions of running a big family and a business.

Thank you also to the people who form a seemingly unending silken web of support and play: Adam Bauer, Yelena and Al Klairmont, Robert Gettleman, Maya Katherine, Leigh Weinraub, Carl Haney, Wendy Hoffmann, Anthony Sandberg, Sean Ahearn, David Ewing Duncan, Cristina Star, Christopher Tompkins, and Hooman Khalili. To John McCaull, who changed everything for me, for better or for worse. A profound thank you to my son and business partner, Kyle Sleeper.

And to my mother: had we only healed the right person, maybe you would still be with us. May the dream of a less violent, more connected world be realized.

San Francisco, 2016

CONTENTS

PROLOGUE

IN 2004, I arrived in a small auditorium on the Monterey coast to attend the annual TED conference, at that time a smallish gathering of polymaths interested in big questions. It was still two years before TED would find itself online and many years before it became a global media powerhouse. Maybe because you enter with the expectation that everyone there will be brilliant and have something amazing to say, it manifests. The TED culture is one in which you proactively open up, introduce yourself, and start asking questions. You enter with the intent to discover the other, which creates more rapid, deeper dialogues on important themes.

The TED theme that year was "The Pursuit of Happiness." The invitation read, in part, as follows:

> ...Maybe we could start doing things a little differently. Maybe, just maybe, we could discover a deeper, longer-lasting, more profound form of happiness. Maybe we could even do this before we ended up mangling our personal relationships and destroying our planet.... I invite you to immerse yourself in the mystery of Happiness. I don't promise she will yield all her secrets. But I'm pretty sure the immersion itself will provoke, intrigue, and delight.

That first day at TED punched me in the gut. I have never felt simultaneously so small and so inspired. It was the first time that I saw one person after another who burned with inner fire and mission. People working on things as diverse as fighting pandemic, improving aging, elevating the slums, building fantastic art structures, exploring space and the oceans. With their work, they were moving the needle for all of humanity. And all in one place! Not segregated into industry specific meetings or single themed conferences.

After just a few conversations, I was sure I had found my people—people who believed that envisioning change or dreaming big was worthy of action and funding, rather than skepticism or scorn. At the time, I was a tech CEO living in Chicago, and a single mom of four: a careerist providing for my family. TED made me step back and ask, "What am I doing with my energy that will have long term meaning? How can I channel my life energy into working on a major challenge facing humanity or the planet?"

The urgent root issues that jumped out at me were climate change, pandemic, economic disparity, and intraspecies violence the violence we do to ourselves and each other).

On climate, I was ill prepared to do anything other than learn and change my own habits. I had no unique insights or unique motivation in that direction. I wasn't a policy maker or an engineer. I could be an activist, but that was about it. On pandemic, public health and economics, I made a similar assessment.

But disconnection and violence, on the other hand, these were things my life had prepared me to deeply understand. Whether it was the chaos of moving more than a dozen times during childhood, my mother's murder, deeply rooted family anger, or witnessing political violence first hand during the Iranian revolution, this was familiar territory. Early violence and early abandonment damages people and family systems, and that damage can persist for decades if not healed. And more than decades: violence and alienation cast long shadows across generations.

I developed a thesis that violence is really the ultimate expression of a more pervasive human problem: disconnection from the self and each other, a root cause of milder forms of suffering such as loneliness and alienation. This disconnection even explains in some ways our collective fractured relationship to the natural environment.

In my experience, the inner life of the self is inseparable from the experience and co-creation of our shared outer world. The two domains are intertwined. The core beliefs we have about ourselves and the people close to us are reflected and magnified in the design of our system. As we shift our interior systems and beliefs, so will the outside world also be changed.

And so, I began to think of the places of my greatest suffering as the places where I might serve. I would devote my life to combating loneliness, anger and violence from the inside out. From here on out, *I would only work on things that reduced the suffering of separation.*

At the same time, I was a few years into studying transformative practices such as yoga, meditation and cognitive behavioral psychology, and had already been asking questions such as: *Who are we really? What are we here to do? How can I live transparently? Where am I authentic, and where am inauthentic? Are the things I have been taught to believe actually the right things to believe—do I really believe them? Could I do things differently?*

I was also healing from my own old injuries and grievances and asking questions like: *Why are people violent? Where do I have a violent impulse? How is the lack of connection related to the impulse to do harm, to others or myself? How does that disconnection show up in the larger society, in our institutions?*

As a child, I sometimes felt very alone in this big world. Yet, even at seven years old, lying alone in silence while staring up at the stars and the moon, I understood that I was somehow "with everything": a part of it, not separate. It wasn't a conscious thought, but rather a sensing. I *felt* the vast peacefulness of the unmitigated universe. *Lonely,* I began to think, is not the same thing as *alone.* As an adult that observation expanded. I noticed that I could be lonely in a room of a hundred people or even in bed with a man I loved. And I can be alone while also being connected, in flow, and creating when there is no one else within a hundred miles. The opposite is also true: it doesn't take proximity to be connected. I don't have to be holding someone's hand. I can be far apart and still communicate and feel the presence of another. The difference rests in my perceptions or state of mind.

The truth I eventually put into words was this: We are always connected—to one another, to the environment, to the universe, even to the past and future. We know that on an atomic level everything is intertwined, and it's no different on the visible scale.

I wondered, why don't we feel this connection more often? My experiences are not unique. Loneliness and alienation are pervasive: there are more people living alone than ever in history, more depression then ever recorded. Why are so many of us unhappy, separated from each other and in many cases separated even from our families? Why do we as a culture emphasize the differences between us, to the point of social and political vitriol, rather than collaboration? Is there something, or many things, in our biology, our culture, that lead us to separation? What does science say? Can we change direction and evolve differently? And if so, how? Disconnection isn't mine alone, and it's also not uniquely yours.

In order to not base my conclusions strictly on my own experience, I started an intense period of inquiry—a decade of experimentation and explorations. In between raising my four kids, along with my husband's two daughters, and working full time, I found myself attending services in dozens of churches and temples and mosques to see that they had in common, studying neuroscience and the brain, visiting pot farms, singing at festivals, studying tantra, crying with life-eligible inmates (life-eligible means you get a sentence of some number of years up "to life" in prison) in a maximum security prison, teaching yoga in a fighting gym and being there with my husband (and our whole family) on what we call now "the cancer experience."

During this exploration, I ended up in a lot of extreme places without having intended to go there. Then I started actively seeking them out, because they are so instructive. The extremes contain all things: joy and euphoria, overwhelming emotional stress, unearthly forms of understanding. Ultimately, deliberately going to places that were outside my comfort zone remade me. The extremes rewired me for greater compassion, and each step emboldened the next exploration.

Asking questions and talking to people from all walks of life also taught me another thing: I was often, *very often*, wrong in my first impressions. When I listened intently to people's stories, in a state of suspended judgment or inquiry, I often realized how my pre-existing biases and stories colored my world and that *they were usually not correct at all*.

Every time I was wrong, the ensuing humility reinforced a new habit: *Ask questions, in as many different ways as possible.*

4

Questions don't have to be asked with words. Inquiry can take the form of looking deeply at a thing, examining it in detail, like an artist who wants to create an exact replica of a painting. When an artist reverse engineers how a painting was made, every brush stroke goes under the microscope. Inquiry can be actively seeking new experiences—especially traveling and seeing first hand that there are other ways to do things. Or approaching strangers, introducing oneself, and making small talk, because small talk often leads to real talk: a dialogue about life, values, worldviews.

The broader my exposure to different people and cultures got, patterns emerged, such as where there was usually joy and where, consistently, there was separation. In almost every place I visited, in addition to beauty, there were people separated from each other—angry, blaming, isolating, discontented. I tried not to be solely an observer, keeping my distance as a researcher would, but to accompany each experience with a reflection of how *I* was like that person, how are we the same. Where do my own walls go up, where do my biases take over, where do I disconnect, and what can I do about it?

The way we live and work together now is very new in human history. We are all part of a massive uncontrolled social experiment that is clearly succeeding in some areas and failing in others. We don't know the impact of the major changes in the way we are living today will impact us: Will it work to have our kids raised by people outside our extended families, outside the tribe? Will it work to feed people 100% packaged foods? Will public education work? Will our brains and bodies be forever changed by technology? Can we drive to work in the dark and come home in the dark and still feel like we have responsibility to a community, or even to each other?

Even if these questions have not been answered in macrocosm, through large-scale research or experiments, we can ask in microcosm: "Is this working for me and those I love?"

That we can answer. Redesign of our systems won't be coming quickly from the body politic or the voting booth. While waiting for those mountains to move, we can make the choice to create change in our own lives and our own immediate surroundings. We begin the redesign from the inside out—from our own values and needs. We don't have to passively wait for it to shift.

Often, people only seek new answers when they are in acute pain. How many of us have embarked on a spiritual journey only after a traumatic loss, such as the loss of a loved one, or an illness, or money or a beloved parent? Yet, searching can also be inspired by a desire to create more joy and fullness of the experience of living. After all, a rising tide lifts ALL boats. Your joy is contagious. Yes, I want to avoid my own suffering and create more joy, but I also want to find out how the whole world can be more connected, loving, tolerant, less neurotic, less violent, less self centered—and more fun. How it can work better for every one of us. Increasingly I feel that this isn't just a nice-to-have— it's a must-have. The things we face as a species really don't know national borders: we have to get better at collaborating.

I think I was duped, and that many of us were, into believing we are separate. That view has been ported into the larger world: in the anger and violence of armed conflict, into identity-based politics, into a strained relation-ship with Earth. Yet, a different view is not only possible, it is happening now, all over the planet.

This book is meant to start conversations on how we can reconnect, how we can live in inquiry. I tell some of my own story, and the stories of others, adding in some of the science and data around connection and disconnection. You will meet many people as you come along on this journey: Valeska and Mia, my German grandmothers; Mark, the lanky New Zealander whose work is the trunk of Western yoga's family tree; Chuck, who has rescued hundreds of dogs and in doing so, rescued himself from a cycle of violence; founders of intentional communities, pioneers in the redesign of work. Out of respect for my kids, I've left them largely out of the story, but they are incredible, kind, funny, and thriving in their lives and loves and very much living in rich net-works of their own.

I believe we can reclaim a deeply connected, present life. We start inside of our own selves by excavating disconnecting beliefs and mastering our minds and emotions, and from there we can move to the outside, developing richer connection in our love relationships, families and institutions. We can live together better. Thank you for joining me on the journey.

To one world, indivisible,
CMM

FROM THE INSIDE

The First Separation

He inhaled for the first time then
Exhaled a great wailing protest with all the force
His almost 11 pounds could muster.
In a daylong, entranced collaboration
Of effort and pain with the woman who grew him in her body
His overly large head was squeezed to a fine point
His body twisted, his lungs massaged,
until he was finally expelled, and with unceremonious finality
the cord was cut.
Now, he was a person.
Helpless, but a person nonetheless
life's own fierce and hungry mandate
to just keep going—
– CMM

Out of the woods

I WAS BORN early, underweight, nicknamed Maus, and left to my own devices. I watched the world from my Maushole and my questions grew bigger, until the questions outweighed the fear. I have been on the road more or less ever since. Maybe, if you don't believe your own version of the truth, you have to keep looking.

At four, I took myself for a walk around the neighborhood in matching raincoat and boots, holding a see-through bubble umbrella and singing my way through puddles to see what the rain was like *in it,* instead of watching it from the window. This solo excursion was rewarded by a belt whipping. Whatever I had done, all I knew was that it was very, very bad. But it did teach me that I could play and experience fun and joy by myself. The trick would be not making anyone mad. I'd have to follow my parents' rules, which generally involved a lot of sitting and moving at alternately designated times, unless they were fighting or looking at each other in that locked-eyes way, like two animals warily watching and circling each other. Their behavior was unrelated to anything that was happening in the lives of their children, my brother Dirk and me; when they were arguing, they ignored us completely, giving us a free pass to do whatever we wanted.

During these times, Dirk and I would join the other neighborhood children outside, and march around, self-governing like the *Lord of the Flies.* Or we'd escape to the backyard swings or to the basement, turn on *The Brady Bunch* or *Speed Racer* and sit nearly on top of one another until the fighting was over.

When our parents fought, a force field overtook them, something magnetic. A switch flipped, and there'd be nothing they could do to hold back. At least, that's how it felt—as if their conscious selves were gone. When they came to and remembered they had children, they'd pretend to be normal people again. "Hey, who wants ice cream?" my dad would say and pile us into his too-small-for-a-family black Mustang. Off we would go to Mitchell's Ice Cream Parlor. *We're all okay, right?*

From my grown-up vantage point, I have compassion. My dad was working full time while getting his Masters degree. My German mother was in a new country, isolated in the suburbs, two little kids—but back then? Just so much fighting.

Once, when I was seven and doors were slamming upstairs, I took a pillow, blanket, a Chrissie doll (the kind that grows her own hair), and some chocolate bars that were hidden in the storage closet, put it all in a wagon, and exited through the garage. Determined never to come back, I walked several blocks before I stopped to rest under a stop sign. There was a new development going in across the way. They had bulldozed some roads and lots, which temporarily turned the Midwestern prairie into the canyons of the west, the Great Wall of China, the Swiss Alps for all Our Gang. Iridescent rainbow wheat and wild carrots and wild strawberries and baby bunnies who hadn't figured out yet that they were doomed held on in that terrain and made it into a wonderland of small surprises. I took myself there, put down the blanket and pillow, ate the chocolate, and fell into a deep sleep.

A chill woke me. The stars were out and the moon was out and there was the sweet hum of crickets, but mostly there was silence. I could have stayed forever if not for the cold, and a low-grade worry about my baby brother back home.

When I returned to the house, it was lit up; a police car hulked in the driveway. I don't remember anything after that, except for a feeling of surprise and shame.

Summers were different. Some years we went to Oma Mia's in a little German town where my family had lived for generations. Nestled up in a feather bed in the little bedroom at the top of the stairs, I would wake up to the sound of church bells ringing from the tower of the Propsteikirche of St. Petrus and Andreas. Even today they chime endlessly before Mass, calling all in to worship. The bells ring as they have for 800 years, as if GPS and well-marked, well-lit roads have never come to be. During the winter, they sound for ten straight minutes at six p.m., to guide travelers to town if they've stayed out too long and can't find their way back in the snow and dark.

At Oma Mia's, the windows were left wide open all night. Cool summer air from the surrounding forest descended on the town. My great-grandmother rose every morning, unpinned her Marcel wave, put on a shirtwaist dress with a belt and hard shoes and began the day, ruling the place with an iron fist, nagging and picking on my grandmother until evening.

My grandmother, a sort of elf in matron's clothing, would grab my hand. We'd find a secret place in the garden, somewhere between the stone wall and the roses, or tucked behind a gnarled tree where we were out of sight of the kitchen. We'd sit in the mossy moistness telling jokes and making up stories about people or things we'd seen together. *Where did Frau Thiele get her little dogs? Why did Frau Ottminghaus use that ridiculous hair color? What would she look like if it were bright pink instead? How many magic creatures like fairies or gnomes did we think could live in a garden this size?* We'd stay in our hideaway until it was time to go back to household work.

These two women, collectively known as the Omas, handed me coins to get fresh rolls from the market or assigned me an errand at a neighbor's place. My outings were informative. I met everyone in the town—I was Monika's American daughter, a special badge when there was nothing else special about me. I was average in size and complexion, a white girl with short legs and lacking any sort of outstanding athleticism in a land of long limbed Aryans. I didn't play any instruments or have any unique talents. I was just a kid who existed; that was the pervasive feeling of my youth.

Meanwhile, back home, the Omas ironed everything that was washed—including handkerchiefs—and in the kitchen, they peeled dozens of potatoes and cooked various saucy and delicious things. They maneuvered around the traditional European kitchen, kneeling on the mustard and flax upholstered benches to set the long table with fresh pressed linens and bone china selected to match the meal or the season. Everything had a place, and everyone had a role in this old-fashioned household.

Every day of the week my uncles, their wives, some older cousins, the old Opa, and my brother Dirk and I were called to table for this meal and an ongoing accounting of our moral and ethical unfolding. The food wasn't complicated, but at one o'clock in the afternoon a three-course meal would be served, along with argumentation. Meals were never peaceful; nor were we exploring deep, lifelong-pursuit type questions. Rather it was an exercise done in the service of analytical thinking and intellectual acuity. For example, the purchase of a giant new freezer resulted in three days of lunchtime conversation on whether premade frozen meals were moral, how freezing food impacts farmers, and whether the food would still have nutrition.

While being exhorted to think for myself and being taught that it was paramount to defend my thoughts with logic and evidence, there was a secondary message that "loud and insistent" goes a long way in creating emphasis and deflecting criticism. While facts were good, eye-rolling was an equally accepted debate tool. Whether we were discussing the evils of frozen food, taxes or why my uncles would never go to church again, Dirk and I—the only children at the table—were encouraged to share what was on our minds. "How was your day?" was not a rhetorical question. It was an invitation—indeed, an expectation—to give specific examples of people we met or things we learned. It was an invitation to think and communicate. Though sometimes overwhelming, it felt like an embrace.

Alternating summers, my brother and I were mailed off to our other grandparents, who took us to their little place on a five by seven mile island in the upper reaches of Lake Michigan. Sometime in the late 1950s, they had built a two-room cabin and an outhouse on the old property, lugging smooth lake stones up the hill for the fireplace. The island was dominated by the no-nonsense, scrubbed work ethic of Scandinavian immigrants and the palpable legacy of the Potawotami Indians.

Ellen—we didn't call her "Grandma"—was sort of shackled to the place in summers, a city girl through and through. She would sit in her Jackie O dresses and horn-rimmed rhinestone glasses on an aluminum folding chair, smoking and reading, while my grandfather did whatever he did, which, to my brother and me, were some pretty awesome things: fishing with a wooden pole, dangling from a tree limb to get the perfect drop into a swimming hole, carefully peeling bark off the white birches to use as paper or to make into toys. He taught us that poison ivy has three leaves on a stem, with the red dot in the middle and a powdery coating on the underleaf—we could check it with a branch if we weren't sure.

Once, he woke us in the night, quietly rustling us from the aluminum cots we slept on next to the kitchen stove. He held a flashlight in his hand and his forefingers to his lips and whispered, "Put on your boots and one of the warm coats. Let's go see some magic." We closed the cabin's knotty pine door softly, pulling our coats tighter around us, padded by the stand of cedars and pines, past the rock painted with the words *Sans Souci*, French for "without a care," and then onto the paved road. We walked a while, past the curve, into a big clearing. He directed our eyes to the North. Dancing in the sky was a light-show of green and gold, spiking like fireworks.

"That," he said, "is the Aurora Borealis, the crown of the Earth. It's light at play with the Earth's magnetic fields, up around the North Pole. You can only see it a few days a year up here. When I was a boy, I thought it was fairies and gremlins or a doorway to other places."

After some silence, he drilled us again on the summer night sky. "Where is the Big Dipper? Can you find Polaris, the North Star? Orion's belt? Cassiopeia?"

When my own children were babies, I made a lullaby about that night:

Aurora Borealis
The Northern Lights
Halo over the planet
When the season's right
You see the Big Dipper
And the North Star
Carry you homeward
Wherever you are . . .

The bud:
Do we have intrinsic or extrinsic worth?

The bud
stands for all things,
even for those that don't flower,
for everything flowers, from within, of self blessing;
though sometimes it is necessary
to reteach a thing its loveliness,
to put a hand on its brow
of the flower
and retell it in words and in touch
it is lovely
— **EXCERPT FROM GALWAY KINNELL'S, "St. Francis and the Sow"**

WHERE DOES OUR core worth come from? Is it an intrinsic or an extrinsic sense of worth? Do we believe we are intrinsically valuable, beloved by the mere fact that we are born? Or do we believe that our value has to be earned—that it comes from outside of ourselves?

If we believe that we are intrinsically worthy and have our own sort of expertise and insight, it's easier to respect and trust our own thoughts and opinions: we don't give away our power to others. From deep self-respect, we can clarify our values and figure out our core beliefs based on our direct experiences, and define an authentic life around those values.

Conversely, if we start from a position of believing that we have to earn our worth, and seek constant feedback or reinforcement from others, then we

14

might design a life around others' needs. We might design a life based on the praise and blame game: If you do what I want, I will reward you, and if you don't, I will punish you in some way.

If our value is derived externally, it is easy to lose connection with the self to the point where we don't really know what we really think and believe anymore, and we just accept the status quo.

I learned pretty early on that my value was external (grades, looks, money), and depended on the reflection of others to understand my own identity and worth. When the entire family situation was dissolved and upended, there was no sense of self worth independent of their reinforcement—just confusion.

Interwoven:
How are we related?

MY GRANDFATHER INVENTED a lot, spoke little, and had low tolerance for conflict of any kind. "Petty conflict is beneath all of nature," he told us, and therefore unworthy of his time. His son, my father, did not inherit this temperament. While he was capable of great wonder, he was all too ready to fight to be right. He brought his frustration and anger with what was broken in the world back home with him.

My German mother, in her beauty and wildness and appetite for risk and expansion—she of the bell bottoms and well stamped passport, the six-language-speaking, guitar-playing hippie chick—and my American father, in his duty and rationality and introversion—he of the masters in economics, the thirty-year-corporate career, the regular-bill-paying citizen—fought continually. And when they weren't fighting, they were just apart. My mom traveled back to Germany, my dad worked and trained for footraces. They never did resolve their conflict in values, and eventually called it quits. The divorce was not amicable. It was full of fear and accusation and blame. I was eight. Dirk was four. My father took full custody and lost fifty pounds that he couldn't afford to lose, presumably from the worry, grief, and stress.

My mother, however, in full rejection of the court's visitation orders, just snuck into the house for private powwows and secret planning sessions. Sometimes she would pick us up and take us to her place, a one-bedroom apartment in downtown Chicago, with art that people had gifted to her hanging on the walls. On other occasions, we would play tennis, listen to music, or visit her friends. Our time together was inconsistent, but there was always some kind of contact. She called every day to talk.

When I was 11, she knocked on the front door after school. I knew nothing of the agreements she was violating, the restraining order my father had placed on her. I thought, *You're my mom; of course you can come in.* She walked around the house picking up things—glass paperweights, a newly framed photograph, my dad's glasses, turning them over in her hands—and digging through drawers, reading the return addresses on envelopes. Then we saw a car pull into the driveway. It was J, a woman my father had recently begun dating; I was supposed to go with her to shop for a winter coat.

"Hide me!" my mother said.

Like two best friends sneaking around past curfew, Mom and I ran downstairs to the unfinished basement. We crouched on the cold cement floor, huddling, feeling one another's warm breath in the damp cellar, her suntanned legs peeking out from a long, calico-trimmed denim skirt. Everything in this memory is in snippets of senses: her unpolished toenails and her anxious face and the cement and J. pounding on the door upstairs yelling, *"We're going to be late! Come on, what are you doing? Do I have to call your father?"*

As foolish as it felt once it left my lips, I told my mother, "I have to answer the door, or I'll get in trouble."

"No, you don't have to answer the door. You don't have to go anywhere. I'm your mother," she said.

With all the pounding and the yelling, I just said, "I have to go."

I never saw my mother again.

My mom's visits simply stopped. Where had she gone? I would phone her desperately to an unending ring. I decided to take the train to her apartment in downtown Chicago. I walked toward the lake, looking for her street, asking strangers where it was. Eventually I found the building that looked familiar and got let in by a familiar neighbor. I knocked, but no one answered, so I just sat there and sat there. After hours passed, I decided to head back home.

My father said nothing about Mom's absence until one day, maybe a month later. My brother had just come home from day camp. My father was packing little ceramic things and random articles of clothing—anything attached to my mother—into boxes. And he was crying, something we'd never seen him do before. He sat me down on the edge of the bed and said, "Your mother is dead. She's never coming back." My big, strong dad curled me up in his arms on a flimsy twin bed in a rented house in the Chicago suburbs and wept with his full being.

My mother's death was impossible to understand.

Her body was found by some farmers in a cornfield off the interstate near Zionsville, Indiana. It had significantly decomposed. She was identified by her dental records. Her killer was never found, despite some half-hearted investigations. The police never contacted her German family, who had important information on dates and whereabouts. This was 1977. It was pre-Internet and pre-cell phone; many of the tools we take for granted today were unavailable. The police report, read in the light of current thinking, was misogynist and racist; she hung out with black people; she was divorced; she was reputed to have smoked marijuana. Basically, they wrote her off. Another dead woman.

There was no funeral. There was no therapy. There was just *deal with it*. And so I numbed out, and went on living.

Being labeled:
Becoming the other

WITHIN 10 MONTHS, my dad remarried. Sue was a coworker, a single career woman with a daughter a little younger than me. A few months later, Sue and my dad were employed to install telephone systems for Mohammed Reza Pahlavi, the Shah of Iran, in Tehran. Our newly constituted family of five moved to Iran in the middle of a fomenting revolution. And that was that—mom's death, dad's quick remarriage, the move—we just stuffed it under the rug, and moved on.

When we stepped off the plane in Tehran, there was no comparison to anything any of us had ever experienced before—it wasn't remotely the United States or Europe. From the landscapes to the faces, we were in alien territory. I had a sense of peering through a periscope: I was looking up and out at the world around me, wanting to make meaning out of a new space, but instead discovered more confusion: *What forces were at work, what was going on here?*

The company provided taxi vouchers to travel around town. Unbeknownst to our parents, who were working all day, my younger brother, stepsister, and I used the taxis to explore. We would just dial up for a car, and the drivers would take us anywhere we asked to go, dropping us at a mosque or into the middle of the main bazaar. We learned just enough of the language to be unknowingly dangerous to ourselves. We could order a taxi or see something interesting from the backseat and tell the driver, "Daste Rast" or "Daste Chap"—to turn wherever we wanted. Before we knew it, we could be in a remote part of the city, just three little white kids, uncovered preteen girls and a nine-year-old boy, essentially on our own.

Iran was breathtaking and overwhelmingly beautiful. We slid along blue tiled walls, passed under decorated archways at the central bazaar, crawled into ancient, inviting nooks and crannies. I felt the names of cities, like Isfahan, tingle as they rolled around in my mouth. *IsssssfaHannn*. And yet, everywhere we went, we were pinned, immediately and consistently, as the "other." Women would come and finger my brother's bright blonde hair while we waited for the school bus, and stare at my eyes.

It wasn't all sheer curiosity. I was politically ignorant and oblivious to any potential danger, although I felt the judgment of some strangers and wondered why they seemed to hate us. Why were we getting these sullen stares? They didn't know us. We'd done nothing wrong. The juxtaposition of feeling pure awe of this ancient place and being rejected from it was pointed.

Even in its beauty, there was still much overt violence in Iran. It appeared in the food marketplaces, where slaughtered animals hung before being chosen, cooked, and eaten. It was in political demonstrations and riots and screaming, where effigies of Uncle Sam were burned in the streets. It was in micro-interactions with angry individuals.

The tension and conflict in the overall culture was also clear. The adaptive force, the one vying for change and the conservative force, the one wanting to protect the old ways. The Shah and his supporters (and his violent secret police, but that's another story) were trying to modernize Iran—not just with things such as the telephone infrastructure that my dad and stepmother were putting in, but culturally as well. Western-oriented change was most concentrated around the universities in Tehran, and we didn't live far from them. The Iranian women in my family's friendship circle were going to university or working. They wore blue jeans and didn't cover their heads and bodies.

The other force was the traditional: the women in *chadors* (veils) and the men who wanted fundamentalist Muslim law (*shari'a*) to be enforced.

As the revolution approached, things got hot fast: Expatriate commuter vans were overturned and set on fire. Workplaces and schools were closed. As we lived in the intellectual center, the marches were all around us. We were quarantined to our house during much of the holy month of Ramadan, while angry mobs marched down the street.

While I had seen anger up close before, it was usually directed at something I understood—undone homework or an unwalked dog. In Tehran, I was seeing the same look of fury on men's faces, but I had no idea what they were upset about. The anger was broadly directed at my entire country, there was nothing I could do about it, and that was an awful realization. I don't think my dad or stepmom explained anything to us about the violence. We were kids, so it was their goal to protect us from the "why," keep us safe, and ultimately get us out of there.

The forces of tradition won out. As the Ayatollah Khomeini prepared to return to power, we were evacuated back to the United States in the middle of the night with whatever we could carry. Any friendships were severed. On the day we were evacuated by our caretakers, just before the American hostages were taken by the Iranian government, we were told to lie down in the back of their car and keep our heads down. We were driven to the U.S. Air Force base, where we kids got on a plane full of dependents and were shipped home. My father and stepmother relocated to Thailand in the belief that the upset would be temporary and they could return to work in a few weeks.

My brother, stepsister, and I were sent to our grandparents in Chicago, and were quickly transitioned back into American Civics and *Stairway to Heaven*-themed middle school dances. The environment at home was familiar, but we were fundamentally changed. We now knew that there were thousands of ways to live on this planet and forces at work that were much broader than this narrow suburban lifestyle would ever have shown us.

As a young teen back in my home country, I began processing other examples of violence in the world around me. I began connecting the violence of my mother's murder to the political demonstrations in Iran and seeing them as part of a pervasive net of violence that surrounded us. The summer we returned was also the summer when police began exhuming bodies from serial killer John Wayne Gacy's crawl space—thirty-three young men and boys. The Chicago news channels broadcast the details with gory, sordid sensationalism. Elsewhere, it was IRA bombings and Russians in Afghanistan and Nicaragua and Zulfikar Ali Bhutto and of course the hostage crisis in Iran, which came after we left.

Coming of age for many young women is about coming into sexual consciousness and feminine power. For me, there was that of course, as my body elongated itself, grew cheekbones and curves, but it was also a time of becoming conscious of violence everywhere. This was the pervasive under-current in every newscast, in relationships between people, and even in the relationships people had with themselves.

Moreover, I couldn't get too lost in the archetype of the romantic Tiger Beat swooning girl. I had other things on my mind. My fantasy life was all around love, in the service of stability, and creating home. I bought my own set of Dansk china for my bedroom at fourteen, so I could create a sanctuary where I could eat alone or with a friend without being disturbed: a home within a home that I controlled. I so deeply craved mothering and physical attention that I would spend my afterschool afternoons at my boyfriend's house—30% because I liked him and 70% because his mother treated me like one of her own. I was shocked to see how differently their family unit operated. It felt like a *real* family. This was a whole other way to live.

In those years, I had few ambitions beyond acceptance. I made good grades, I engaged in activities at school, but I was numb to most sensations. I was invited to things, still I felt like an outsider everywhere I went, and found it hard to make real friends. In retrospect, it was probably some PTSD kind of thing—a reaction to many levels of unacknowledged loss.

If you want to see separation in action, go to a public high school cafeteria—it's a theater where students resign themselves to defined roles and cliques, cast micro-judgments on each other's groups and establish what most people perceived as impenetrable borders. The "burn-outs" could never join the "jock" table; the music theater people rarely strayed from each other—people were just running their selected scripts.

Integration and authenticity was rare. There were few people who could own their intelligence, physicality, wonder, doubt and angst and not hide out in a type. This was true not only of students; most of the adult staff too, seemed to step into a stereotype and stay there. I wondered how the few who were open and clear and obviously multidimensional came to be that way—and how those who had already created or accepted an identity that put them in a box might move toward more freedom.

The kids who smoked in the school parking lot, who were drugged round the clock, the actors and punks—those who seemed to have more suffering in their lives, once you saw past their veil of toughness or disinterest—were the ones who, paradoxically, seemed the most present and authentic. The guys throwing footballs and big-manning-on-campus were weaker, in some ways, than those in the disenfranchised group, who showed more vulnerability. But all were in some ways masking their wholeness, and playing to a type.

Choosing to know each other:
Unbiasing

There was a time you let me know
What's really going on below
But now you never show it to me, do you?
— LEONARD COHEN, IN *HALLELUJAH*

WHY DO WE label people? What is the nature of a person, and can we see each other in our wholeness?

At a party, the first thing people often ask is "What do you do?" At best, this is a shorthand way to connect. At worst, it's a way to quickly judge whether to embrace or dismiss a person, or to assess whether they are potentially useful. For example: to me, you're a taxpayer. To me, you're a widget maker. To me, you're a consumer. This is a utilitarian mindset: Do you have utility to me?

By reducing people to a job and encapsulating them, we gain perceived control and utility over others. Non-control is frightening. It's as if we need to say, "I know and understand this object or this person. I have leverage over them. Because I am weaker than the bigness of the universe, I need a way to feel that others are small enough for me to encompass."

This belief allows us to treat others as utility objects, to be used for our own ends. It can lead to dominance hierarchies rather than respectful ecosystems of equals. Dominance and separation attitudes towards others are a breeding ground for all forms of abuse.

For example, we've accepted for many generations that people deserve to live or die based on how closely their ideology matches our own. Ideologies that proffer righteous positions and hold onto them up to the brink of death are passed from person to person like a virus. Whether it's "socialism" or "Catholicism" or "Islam" or "capitalism"—there have been so many persecutions in the name of the "ism"! Philosopher Dan Dennett says the "ism" is the most deadly virus on the planet, killing more people than any form of bacteria. Maybe "isms" are more like coronary disease, the true heart disease of our planet. Ideology-based simplification of the others identity lets us hurt them because they are different from us—we only see that one label.

The tendency to label, describe, or box people in misses the real connection, the real seeing of all people we encounter. Social taxonomy ignores human beings' broad gifts and truths, whether in school, the workplace or a country club.

A person is not an economic unit to be mined for resources; every person is intrinsically valuable and deserves to be treated in a way that will maximize his or her happiness and immersive experience of being alive.

A whole person is whole in mind, body, and spirit. A whole person has multifaceted interests and relationships. A whole person has others she serves or is responsible to, people she cares for and is intertwined with. A whole person has lifespans and phases, and is not the same person from start to finish. She or he has different priorities and gifts in each age.

Not only do we do oversimplify other people, we do it to ourselves. When we meet people, we often present a consumable front, to offer a clear place for the other to "plug in". By presenting one aspect, rather than the whole, it makes it easy to "pitch" ourselves.

Each person is a basket of amalgamations—we can't be put into a library under a classification system. However, taking the time to see someone as an all-around human may be, in part, a function of intimacy and community size. A large community, a corporation, a bureaucracy, a boardroom could never do this; it would not be efficient. And we're steeped in a culture that places tremendous value on efficiency.

The richer version of the party talk, the inquiry, the move to connection, might have this intention: "What do you do? And let me clarify that I don't mean 'what's your job?' I want to know: how do you spend your time? Does it matter to you? Or what *does* matter to you? What do you see and what do you think deeply about when you are not doing other 'stuff'? Is it even possible, in your opinion, to not be doing 'stuff'? I want a true sense of who I'm speaking to. So, what do you do?"

By saying, "I intend to connect to the real person in front of me, to the whole person in front of me, and to make my life about these genuine connections," we can take a step in refuting reductionism, in refuting utilitarianism, and in breaking down the paradigm of widgets and isolated elements.

Think of examples from real life: a young man who is politically liberal, hunts deer, and loves poetry. A woman who is both devoutly Christian and deeply sensual—practices that aren't often paired together in stereotypes. If you accept one-dimensional labeling, then you turn people into flat, cartoon-like objects. This is how I become an "American" in the eyes of Iranian revolutionaries, instead of Christine.

I've found it a lot more time consuming to walk around in the world trying to be truly present to the people we meet in their wholeness. It's a constant practice of being aware of our prejudices and instantaneous judgments, our compulsion to turn people into the "other." To do this on a regular basis, we really have to care about the outcome.

We have to value the idea that a movement based on interconnectedness moves people in the general direction of harmony—within ourselves, with each other, and with the planet. For me, that is an outcome worth caring about. If interconnection were the foundation of our belief system, we wouldn't punch holes in walls, burn effigies of the Other, or slander, exclude, bully or harm. The lonely and alienated would instead feel they belonged, like they had a place to call home.

Flying solo

A S A SPECIES, we've been taught that our natural animal response to danger is fight, flight, or freeze (submit). New gender research suggests that females have two additional potential responses: "tend and befriend." In my still conflict ridden home environment, I tried them all. I couldn't fight my parents, so first I tried flight: At 15, I ran away from home to avoid the ongoing conflicts with my stepmother. It was short lived. I went to a friends' house on the other side of the state, and tried to register myself for school there. The police escorted me home. I didn't return to my parents' house, but spent the next six months until graduation living with my grandmother.

But none of this flailing and running was getting me anywhere. I realized that my only option was to just freeze and submit emotionally—at least until I really *could* leave, on my own terms and without sacrificing an education, so highly valued in my family. I was so motivated by thoughts of escape that I accelerated my schoolwork. I started school at seven in the morning. I took summer classes.

Four weeks after my 16th birthday, I graduated. I went back to Germany for the first time since my mom had died. The instant I got to my grand-mother's, I changed into black parachute pants, put on Joan Jett eyeliner and headed to the local nightclub. The bartender jumped over the bar and walked up to me. "Hey", he said. "I'm Gerd. What's your name?" Two days later, he quit his job. We got on his motorcycle and hit the road.

We went everywhere. We went to the north coast, we went to Amsterdam, we went to some remote part of Denmark, we went up to Lake Como. When we thought we had seen enough of any one place, we picked up the map and pointed. The only thing we fought about was that I couldn't ride on the back of his motorcycle without leaning the wrong way on turns. Otherwise, it was pure, unsupervised freedom. We had almost nothing in common, except this desire to explore.

Finding a path

I'D LONGED FOR the day when I'd finally leave the turbulence of my home and go to college, on my own at last, where of course, everything would be perfect. In these daydreams, I'd picture myself at a prestigious private school, institutions with names that produced murmurs of admiration when dropped in casual conversation. In reality, those schools were out of my reach financially. So at sixteen, I started college at a solid public university in a cornfield.

Even though I was paying in-state tuition, I could never quite make ends meet, no matter how hard I tried. I went to school full time while working three jobs— underage bartender at a local institution that served fish fry and Long Island iced teas for the fraternity and sorority crowd; Jane Fonda-style aerobics entrepreneur; reading tutor in the local public schools. Still, I was coming up short at the end of each month, and I was exhausted. About this time, I ran into an Army recruiter on campus, and by the end of the day, I was enrolled in Military Science 101. I learned how to march, studied military strategy and history, and wore full dress uniform every Friday. Welcome to the world of ROTC, the Reserve Officer Training Corps.

Barely eighteen, I headed to boot camp at Ft. Knox, KY. Kentucky in July is damp red dirt, as if the earth itself was sweating. Summer storms turned trails and roads from hard-pack to clay-slip in a matter of minutes.

The women's barracks were sparse: white frame bunk beds, cement steps, gym lockers. My roommates included a blonde, skinny, foul-mouthed military brat from California; she bunked with a black mother of two babies from Michigan, who cried about missing her kids at least once a day. Wakeup was at four a.m.; we started with calisthenics, followed by eight-mile runs over two hills named Agony and Misery. Food was a lot of white bread and sauces dished out in ladles. Our squads and platoons were mixed genders.

The eight hundred cadets in our class learned to bivouac. We learned to march, rappel, scramble over obstacles. We kneeled in the mud, learned CPR and how to bind a bleeding wound. We learned to assemble, shoot, disassemble, and clean an M-16 rifle, and how to handle a weapon with respect. We learned that every long march is made easier by a cadence and a song— songs that included whiskey and killing and women—which even the 20-year-old feminists among us belted out without hesitation. *Hey, hey, Captain Jack, meet me down by the railroad track, with your weapon in your hand, I wanna be a fighting man— sound off…* We learned to speak Alpha Bravo Charlie Delta. We stood in line a lot. We watched men drive tanks into position. We saw Sun Tzu's *Art of War* given flesh and form.

Once, late in the summer, when it had been raining for days, we were on a three-day campout, with measured rations in cans and limited water. We had iodine drops to purify whatever additional water we might find. We were supposed to capture and skin and cook a rabbit, but no one could get the fire started. By the time of this exercise, while we were still urban or suburban babies on many levels, we were no longer soft. We were lean from intense daily training; we were conditioned, and there was a sort of high-performance glow around our edges. But our physical capacity didn't offset the fatigue of this particular exercise—that was mental. People were grumpy and snapping at each other.

As if in a trance, I climbed up onto a log and gave an impromptu motivational speech. It was wholly unexpected: a sharp change in trajectory that followed me for the rest of my life. That moment may have been my first leadership act.

In basic training, my body changed—*I could run!* My mind changed—*I could survive!* And my belief in who I might become changed, too, because I could lead. For this, I give a giant thanks to the United States Army and its proven principles of character formation in young people.

Yet even while there was much good in the way the military brought people together, I understood that underlying this effort was a mission to prepare for war and killing; that all those guys riding around in tanks and playing with munitions were being trained to use them in a real conflict, *without* the safety latches on.

I completed the training—finishing first of the women and third overall of 800—and my Army dad and granddad were proud. But after two years of preparation for a possible career in military service, I opted out at the end of that summer. These were the Reagan years, between wars, post-Vietnam and pre-Gulf War.

Instead of going into combat, we led covert operations for geopolitical enforcement. Many of my peers did go on to serve: some became Army Rangers and logistics officers. And there were those who went the other way, like the two men who went to prison for using their Ranger skills to pirate drug drops in the Florida swamps. But mostly, my peers served and then went on to be regular citizens. Mostly, they didn't kill. But that does not and cannot change the reality: In basic training we were taught (against, as I would later discover, our nature and our hardwiring) to be in competition, and to prepare to kill other humans. That wasn't a situation I could live with.

Now in a quandary about what to do with my life, I decided to take a break and investigate that very question. When summer training ended, I left to be with my extended family in Europe. While attending university classes in the south of France, I walked every day from Aix-en-Provence to a little village called Tholonet, where Cézanne painted all of those delicious saturated images of sunset-drenched Mont Sainte Victoire. I learned to draw and paint, and perfected my French. When my boyfriend of two and half years came over for Christmas, the Big Question settled itself—at least for the time being. Whatever else I eventually chose to do, I would become a mother first.

We're all just babies

SEAN AND I had met during the first class on the first day of my first year of college. I was taking Modern Dance 101, in a wide-open, luminous mirrored studio. There were 80 women and three men in the class. One of the guys had striking hazel eyes. He was a shiny philosophical lifeguard, who had taken the class to meet girls. It worked. By January, we were sharing a group house, a falling-down Victorian with no heat, with three other people. I was a sixteen year old freshman and he was a 22 year old 5th year senior, bound for law school. The next year, while he pursued his legal studies in the big city, we stayed deeply connected.

I was 18 when we married, and at 19 we had our first child, a son. The others followed: a girl at 20, a son at 22, another at 28.

This rapid family-making wasn't completely thought through. Sometimes I think that the first time since my mother died that I ever truly felt *anything* deeply was when I gave birth to my first son. Instead of postpartum depression, or losing my identity after giving birth, which happens to a lot of mamas, I stepped fully into myself. Mothering came completely and joyfully easy for me—I felt it was what I was made to do with these peasant hips and sturdy disposition, to drop babies in the field and keep working—I never consciously made the connection that all of this was a reaction to my own foundational lack of an intact family to rely on.

Sean and I committed to offer these four beings in our stewardship the best home parents could possibly make—stable and connected and creative and clear, to the best of our abilities. Throughout this baby making, Sean finished law school, and I finished college, with a BA in International Relations, then eventually grad school.

We bought a house: a 1910 cedar shake foursquare with a big front porch and a sleeping porch in the back. It hadn't been touched or maintained since 1945. The kitchen "island" was an upended cable spool, and the original cast iron sink was still mounted on the wall. We stayed up nights fixing the cabinets and sanding the floors while the babies slept. We tried to make it perfect. We painted rose-colored walls, and planted perennial gardens. We did what I now call, in light of everything that's since happened, "stenciling the drive-way." That is, we worked on the decorations of life, not the bones or the architecture. This activity was coming from a place of stuffing things down— of being driven, not driving.

While finishing school I trained my body into a size 2, made perfect meals, dressed the children in French cotton, mixed homemade baby food and created handmade Halloween costumes. I thought if we just worked harder, we could have it all: a house full of happy babies *and* clean closets, a new car *and* a full bank account, opera tickets *and* church tithing. I couldn't see at that time why happy babies, paid bills and clean closets are oxymorons unless you have full time household help. We were stretched very thin.

There were times when our kids seemed like extensions of us. We'd take pride in their accomplishments as if they were somehow adding to our own value. We held the kids up to unreasonably high standards, passing on the values we'd inherited. And through it all, while seemingly together on the outside, on the inside I was still confused and angry a lot of the time.

Conditioning and deconditioning

WE CONDITION OUR children sometimes unconsciously. When I reward good behavior, or punish bad behavior, it's a fine line between the behavior and the person. In the process of teaching our children to decide what is right and wrong, we can offer them the understanding that they, at their cores, are inherently pure and valuable, or we can teach them the opposite, and condition them to bend to our will.

In our house, we took pride in their accomplishments—which reinforced a sense in them of being valued for these accomplishments, not for who they are. It's not done with bad intent. But would our children really disappoint us if they were just themselves?

My eldest son told me recently that he never felt like he was good enough. He could do his best, but even then I always wanted more from him. I was stunned when he told me that my encouragement came across not as, "You are great just as you are," but as, "this is another step in your development." My expectations in and of themselves made him feel he was never good enough. Our pride in him wasn't a sharing of his current joy, merely a precursor-in anticipation of his eventual greatness. He felt that his successes somehow mattered more when they were a reflection of how we were doing as parents. How do we communicate to our children, "You are just amazing right now," instead of "You are so amazing, and it's just another step on the path to Harvard."

Ironically, this kind of praise teaches our children that they should be "*special.*" So acknowledging that while yes, they're as unique as snowflakes, the idea that we can be elevated (or diminished) by what we do or don't do if we just work hard enough arises from an external conditioning that values "specialness." Everybody *is not* special, and everybody *is* special, in that everyone is a unique set of experiences and perspectives and gifts. And everyone is also the same; no one is better than anyone else. We are simply who we are, learning and growing. Imagine if no one was getting celebrated or elevated. It's not sad, it's liberating! Explore, live, experience! This is of course not only about our kids: as adults, our work is to free ourselves from unnecessary conditioning and limitations so that we can be our own best selves.

If you were raised this way, relearning your own intrinsic worth is completely possible. Depending on the amount of occlusion (physical, emotional or spiritual injuries one has endured), seeing your own worth and feeling good about yourself can be an instant of grace, or it can be a continuing process of practices and healing. We aren't doomed to be stuck—rather we are built to heal and to keep growing. We just need the right medicine and tools.

Intrinsic value is not something that is told to us. It has to be experienced. Our body has to know. We have to embody our worth, and feel it first hand; it's foundational to reconnecting to our own truth. We begin with some simple questions: What do I feel? What do I believe? What do I desire? What am I here to do? Where do I treat myself with less than impeccable respect or self-love, and how can I shift those habits? What have I been taught about love and worth, and are those beliefs I can change?

When we know our own unconditional worth—we might just be able to extend that to others. From our core true self, we can step into a new relationship with others. We can be of singular strength, and a flowing, aligned part of the collective: *connected but not subsumed.*

We might then love *them* unconditionally. We might just let the people in our lives be themselves. We might say: "I don't want anything from you. You don't have to be any particular way to make me happy. I will love you where you are."

The long shadows of anger

MY FATHER WAS often disgusted with people; nobody could ever do enough. When things didn't happen according to his expectations, stated or unstated, he would break stuff and pound the walls and tell us to "up our game." He didn't hold back.

One night when I was about 14, my father returned home from work expecting the spaghetti to be ready and on the table. He and my stepmom were on a rigid schedule at that time, and we were expected to obey a similarly strict list of chores throughout the day. When something wasn't done, he felt disrespected and ignored—and while it made no sense to us, his rage sometimes went out of control. That Night of the Spaghetti, he punched his fist through the drywall. Then, over and over, like punctuation, his hand ploughed into the hole. He would say something, and he would punch the wall. He'd say something else for emphasis, and he would punch the wall again. We watched, shocked and confused, with our jaws dropped.

My father's life was routine: He was on the same exact schedule every day, the same exact train every day, the same ritualistic bill paying, the menus all the same, week after week (fish sticks on Tuesday, meatballs on Wednesday, macaroni on Thursday). He became entrenched. His worklife became about his pension and savings and his planned retirement. *Is this all there is?* He felt disrespected, angry and bored.

Even as a kid, when you watch someone act like that, you want to know: Where is your joy? Where is your excitement? What do you want to do? Even with a family and community and interests, somehow my father often seemed isolated and unhappy.

In my late twenties, when my everyday life included my own rigid schedule—caring for four young children, an older, needy house, a demanding career, pervasive money challenges, and existential doubt—it became clear that I was my father's daughter.

Small frustrations would build over time, rising closer to the brim, my stress levels spiking. When the pressure exceeded capacity it would surge into anger, and then rage. There was no warm-up. There was no indicator of how intense it would become. I never knew when the anger was coming; neither did anyone else. Even if triggered by something small, my reaction would be disproportionate. If I asked eight times for the clothes to be put away and it remained undone, I would stop asking. I would start screaming and slamming doors.

I'd be sweet, wonderful, wonderful, give, give, give—and then, suddenly, I'd lose it.

This was scary, to me and my family. They could feel it build but couldn't name it. They described it as a sense that I was about to blow. I rationalized that if I didn't hit anybody, didn't hurt anybody physically, it was acceptable.

I got to the point of breaking things only once. Triggered by what I saw as a betrayal, I broke every picture of my husband and me—every single framed picture of the two of us. I slammed them into a pile on the floor. It felt fantastic. It felt like a magnificent release, a sense of relief. Those objects had their own magic and, by breaking them, it felt like I was breaking some bond. In that moment, I could understand why people beat people up, or why they hit things or mutilated their bodies. I looked at that pile of broken glass, frames and pictures, and felt like my pain had been transmogrified into the physical world. There was tangible, material evidence of how bad I had felt inside. There was no one else there; no one had witnessed this disaster; but the power in it was clear.

But once that rush was gone, I had to clean it all up. I had to deal with the mess. The release was temporary, and I was just as mad a week later. One could get to the point, I understood, where there was nothing left to break.

When we possess self-awareness, we can choose what patterns to repeat in our lives and in the lives of our children. For a long time, I had little self-awareness. I couldn't pause and notice that my heart rate was rising, that my breath was short, that my thoughts were racing. I couldn't call out fatigue or hunger or sadness. I couldn't interrupt the cycle *because I wasn't paying attention*. Moreover, I wasn't even questioning my behavior—it just seemed normal, based on what I'd experienced growing up

I often tried to redirect this bad energy into movement, and then into functional activity. If I was *really* mad, I would paint a room or rearrange all the furniture or go through the entire house and organize all my children's closets in one day. Or, I would stomp out at four in the morning and go for a ridiculously long bike ride, until I felt grounded again.

Then, I found sports. I decided to try tennis, mostly for exercise and to have a game or sport that I could carry into later life. I started taking lessons, and I loved it: the thwack of the strings on the ball, the sweat, the pace. I would go hit that ball with grunts and hollers and all kinds of outsized power. There were demons hissing and hollering in each swing.

My coach, Pietr, a big strong former Polish pro, asked me one day, "Where is this coming from in you?"

While there was true delight in the strategy and skill to play well, this expulsion of force wasn't driven by love for athleticism or the release of endorphins or a burning need to expend calories. It was driven by anger. I had never found an outlet for anger until I got physical. Anger could fuel play. Tennis was teaching me how to expel the anxiety and anger on a day-to-day basis, quickly, with one solid whack of the racket. Hitting took something from my body and expelled it and released it into the air to dissipate, for a few hours at least. I wasn't *curing* my problem; I was just moving it out of the way for the time being.

When Pietr thought I was ready, he put me in a doubles match. It did not go well. To be a successful doubles player, you have to be in constant communication with your partner. In order to get access to the bigger playing field, you have to collaborate well; you can't try to prove yourself or try to be better than your partner. It's a dance: *You are moving forward; I am going back. You are going to the right; I am going to the left. Okay. I got it. I got the net. Go. Alright, you hurt your ankle; okay, let me cover both sides while you walk it off.* You look at the other person and know whether they are going to rush the net or move back and open up the court. Without coordination like that, you will fail.

And I did. After the first match, I was furious with myself for letting down my partner, and it showed. It wasn't that I couldn't play tennis; it was that I couldn't communicate.

Pietr pulled me aside. "You have this thing about disappointing others, Christine, and we are not going down that road," he said. "You are going to play singles. I am going to work with you, and we are going to see what happens."

Slowly, during our practice time, I became aware of the power behind the negative energy rising in my body. The emotions I couldn't express with rational discussion and constructive resolution were being released as physical energy. A new thought began to form: *What if I could harness this energy and redirect it?*

Concentrating on the game of tennis on the court, and consciously recognizing my inability to communicate, shed some light on other disconnections. If I was having trouble communicating where I was on the court, how was I "playing" at home—in my marriage or at work?

The tennis training acted as a form of therapy. I came to realize I was dogged by the feeling that I wasn't doing things right in many areas. Perfect was the standard. I always had to be doing more, even when there were literally no more hours in the day. It would take either a dose of grace or much, much effort to stop a belief so deeply ingrained and to remake myself anew.

In general, all of us do the best we can with what we've been given, what we've seen and experienced, and where we are in our self-development.

Sean and I had already been trying for more equanimity, peace, love and connection. Our shingled Cape Cod house, with the big front porch, was filled with reminders that that our family was about love, not anger. We painted murals in the boys' room of idyllic, peaceful scenes. I littered the place with pillows with sweet sayings: like "Love You More" stenciled in black ink on white canvas duck. We acquired bookshelves from a rummage sale for our daughter's room, stained them peony pink, and on the edges of the shelves, in gold metallic paint, hand-lettered the fruits of the spirit: love, joy, peace, patience, kindness, goodness, faithfulness, gentleness and self-control, repeating each word as a mantra. At night, before bed, we would repeat them as an invocation: What is the fruit of the spirit? Love, joy, peace, patience and kindness were about as far as the kids got. No one ever made it to self-control.

Including me.

Throughout all the challenges, there was a weak but constant signal, a quiet call to the sacred, that appeared sporadically on the surface in a burst of gratitude—but not in a visible consistent arc. It was not something I experienced deep in my body. But it was definitely there. (Someone told me much later that once you hear the ringing bell, the pull to the sacred, you are going there—it's just a matter of how hard and how long you resist.)

Nature was always there. Our family would go into the woods at all times of the year, at all times of the day. The little nature center in our town rented out cross country gear, and with a baby on my back and the older ones trying their hardest on tiny skis, our two white wolf dogs running ahead, we would come up over a rise just as the sun slanted in exactly right to make the crust on the snowfall a crystal prism. We would go deep down into the ravines and climb on the ice floes.

One day in particular, when the trillium blossom spread a carpet across the whole wood, we went out early in the day for a hike with my friend Berend, who was visiting from Germany.

The children were laughing and playing, and he asked, "Why are they so noisy?"

"Well, they are kids," I said.

He replied, "No, that's not why. You have to teach them to listen, even in nature."

"You're just being German," I told him. "They're kids. Let them play."

But he insisted, "Seriously, try it. See what happens when you ask them to get quiet and to listen to nature."

So we huddled them up, and Berend used the opportunity to teach them what a poisonous mushroom looked like compared to a non-poisonous mushroom, and that they could tell immediately that any mushroom that is pointed a certain way, even if it may not be poisonous, was definitely not edible. So he was talking and then he said, "Shhhh. Everybody, shhhh. What do you hear?"

They closed their eyes, and they started to listen.

So we made that our thing. If we were out and someone saw or heard something beautiful, anyone could speak up: they'd go, "Shhhhh," and we would hush each other while the person who started the hushing pointed out what they wanted us to see or hear.

In this way, my children learned nature. They learned the wildflowers, and to tell the exact time the seasons were changing. To tell time by the position of the sun. Whether it was the ice crystal palaces of the hardwoods in winter, or the August lakefront, all humid sand and alewives and seventeen-year cicadas, or the ravine and field dress in autumn leaves, nature was a call to remembering.

And we went to church. There was the stillness of the darkened sanctuary at midnight on Christmas Eve, under candlelight, the little girls in velvets with lace, the sleepy-eyed toddlers quiet in surrender. A mother-daughter duo in the balcony raining "Cantique de Noel," better known as "O Holy Night," on the opened ears below. The part where they sing, "Truly, He taught us to love one another/ His law is love and His gospel is peace"—that got me, every time.

Our family went to church a lot—not just on Christmas and Easter—in the hope that our children would gain vision in an area where we ourselves had grown up blind. We wanted them to know the language and the stories and the meaning of the Judeo-Christian heritage, so that they would have a platform and a vocabulary of spirit. And we wanted them to feel some sense of belonging, of being part of the mystic. We were truly involved; it wasn't superficial. We ran the nursery, sang in the choir, led adult education, and attempted to internalize a mature concept of God and faith.

But it wasn't working in my daily life. I wasn't taking Sunday into Monday. I wasn't even taking Sunday into Sunday. I would sit and fidget with the kids and make mental lists of what wasn't done and try hard to focus. I would get itchy in the pews. I was in argument with the prayers, with the paternalism and the conformity and the sense of being a good girl on the outside while feeling wild on the inside. Such loving people, such beautiful music, such simplicity—I heard the words, but couldn't feel them. I couldn't bend my beliefs into a container that worked, and just choose to agree with this part of the Bible, and disagree with that part. I will love the teaching of love your neighbor as yourself, but I not believe that a female has no place in its hierarchy. I was trying hard, but just couldn't agree.

Furthermore, the mainline church wasn't a gospel church where we could move and dance and shake and be in our bodies and celebrate. I was supposed to sit still. They call the Presbyterians "The Frozen Chosen" for a reason. But for me, it was just sitting, without the stillness. Every time we'd start to pray, we'd get a maximum of two minutes before they would interrupt us with organs or some other noise. It was neither embodied prayer, nor meditation.

Anything that might have wanted to come to the surface was immediately pushed away. But isn't that a vital part of prayer, I protested? To listen to what the spirit is trying to tell you? Instead, we were never fully allowed to be quiet; there was no space in which to listen. In my experience with traditional church, there was admonition, instruction and worship, there was thank you, and there was please forgive me. That is all good, but there was neither embodied celebration nor space for listening. It's not that a lack of still prayer and listening, also known as meditation, is exclusive to Christianity; but it's not an extended part of most Christian services.

One fall Sunday, when I was organizing adult education for our church, we brought in a guest teacher, Brother Wayne. Brother Wayne taught us a Christian meditation practice called *Lectio Divina*. It's rarely practiced in modern churches. We each simply opened the Bible, found a place, held our fingers on that place and read it over and over and over to ourselves. Then we closed the book, meditated on that passage and tried to capture its essence and meaning in our own lives. I had been waiting to listen for so long. In the quiet created by Brother Wayne's meditation all kinds of questions arose.

How often in regular life did I pause to ask questions that mattered: Is what I am doing still good for me? Am I serving well? Should I still be eating this food? Should I still be spending my money in this way? Did I ever just pause and ask, is this habit still right? When I got quiet, the questions were big ones. Why am I doing what am I am doing? Why do I show up and do the things that I am doing in my life? I started to see that I was continuing on an automatic routine without knowing why.

Wake up calls

AT 32, WHEN I was the age my mother was when she was killed, and my daughter was 11 (the age I was when my mother died), I kind of froze. What do I do now? How do I raise my daughter now? I had been without guidance from age 11 on, in terms of being a girl or a woman, and I had little idea what to do.

At the same time, I realized I could be dead tomorrow. I could walk out the door like my mother did, and someone could slam my head against the wall and throw me into a cornfield and it could all be over. There was no boundary between me and death. We are living, and then we are dying. It could come at any moment.

And I thought, *don't miss this, don't miss your life.*

Until that point, I had just been accumulating skills. I had learned how to be successful. I was the chief marketing officer of a company, I was efficient and confident, I could run a big household.

When I had my moment of "don't miss your life" clarity, all of that fell away. It was as if a curtain was lifted. I was so sad when I saw the materialism, the objectification and shallowness in my life, the doing and going, the constant striving for external approval with no internal point of reference—and the most painful place of all—the increasingly distant relationship with Sean.

We were playing roles that we didn't inhabit. It had been years since we'd had a real conversation. We cared for and played with the children and updated the house and had sex and went to parties with our friends. We earned our degrees and made more babies and the basement flooded and soaked the laundry once a week, and there was an ever-increasing herd of animals, and we were both playing at what we thought a happy and successful family looked like. Sean, a former East Asia studies and philosophy major, who went to law school to make a difference in the world, was now a personal injury lawyer, socking his big settlements into increasingly addictive behavior. I was redecorating the house and buying new clothes and running a business, while that kid inside of me was trying to fill some deep need for mother love.

I wanted to ask him, *what are we doing? Are we performing for each other? Are you putting on a show for me? Am I still supposed to be the perfect wife? Are we just acting to keep each other happy, or are we being real?*

During this time period, I often didn't want to go home. His behavior was becoming more erratic. He'd paint the same corner of our basement different colors for nights on end, and he wasn't sleeping. He was hoarding, going on outings in which he would buy out all the ivory-handled canes in Chicago thrift stores, or come home with boxes and boxes of vintage books. Once he unloaded several truckloads of wooden chairs, in various states of neglect. I remember one Christmas morning, opening tens of thousands of dollars of gifts when we were late on the mortgage. With four kids, the house and my responsibilities at work, we needed to be aligned more than ever. Instead, I had the sense that he was going, going, nearly gone, into a mysterious netherland, deep in the resources of his own mind.

We went to a counselor. The counselor suggested he go and see a psychiatrist. The doctor began treating him with a cocktail of pharmaceuticals, one of which was Adderall. And then where was my friend? Lost to some amphetamine-induced psychosis. Where was the beautiful papa and inventor of the Black Vantastic (a car that looked remarkably like our black Mazda MPV, with the added features of being able to fly, tell moral stories, and often save the day)? He was buried deep in his own mind's grooves, unreachable.

There are so many places to go, if only we can jump over the image we have been projecting. There are so many ways to leave behind the exhaustion and fatigue of living a role and suffering in this quiet hell of need.

In the middle of this confusion, we met for lunch, between meetings, at Blackbird, in Chicago's West Loop. It was the day after his birthday. We'd been married 15 years. By then, Sean had turned to drugs and bad dealings to manage his own shadows. I said, "You know, you can do whatever you want to do in life. If you want to be a short-order cook—you love to cook for people—you can do that. You love knick-knacky things. If you want to have a gift shop with little elves and fairy trinkets because it brings you joy, you get to choose that." *You can do anything,* but you have to change what you are doing *now* to save yourself.

In a rare moment of vulnerability, he broke down. "I can't choose at all. I have no choice in anything," he said. "What would people think of me?"

It was silence after that. There was something else driving him, something unspoken—the money, the suits, the toys. We had both gotten a glimpse behind the masks, and what I saw behind his wasn't in alignment with who he'd been in his younger years, when his ideals were intact. There seemed to be nothing else to say.

In that moment, we had true compassion for one another, and yet our trajectory was fixed. We wouldn't be able to work it out; we just didn't have the capacity. I would find a way to some better way of living and being—to deeper connection, ease, authenticity and freedom—for all of us. I couldn't anticipate what the way out would be. But one night in Chicago, not long after, it was handed to me.

THE POISE OF THE SOUL

Finding savasana

WHEN I was 22, with 3 kids under 4, I went to business school, then immediately started working in high demand jobs in industry. When the tech boom of the late 90s hit, I started a company with several colleagues. In no time we'd raised millions in venture capital, and were working crazy hours to execute against the commitments we'd made. It was an insanely challenging time.

After a particularly long day in this spell of dot-com craziness, I was walking on a crowded street to catch a commuter train when I saw my old friend Daniel. Daniel was always a person I respected. He had a ready smile. He was self-contained, a loving husband and father and very accomplished professionally—at that time he was CEO of a public company, making all manner of kitchen gadgets.

That night, he was shining. It looked to me like he had shed layers of himself; he was carrying no burden.

"What happened to you? You look fantastic!" I exclaimed.

He responded in an instant. "Yoga happened to me, and *you* look terrible. So, you're coming with me this Friday."

That's how my "way out" presented itself—as a way in.

Yoga is sometimes called "Poise of the Soul." Poise is equilibrium, readiness, balance, steadiness, stability, suspension between states of motion. Poise does not freak out over laundry, talk too much, go 90 miles an hour to make it to a meeting, or accidentally break things due to inattention.

I went to Daniel's yoga class. After a great struggling 75 minutes of a vigorous athletic form of structured yoga postures all linked together and led by the breath (we were practicing a form called Ashtanga yoga), the class arrived at *Savasana*, corpse pose, where we lay on our backs, arms outstretched, palms up, legs extended, letting all of our muscles relax, allowing our bones to sink into the floor, in a sort of half-state between sleeping and waking, a state of deep aware stillness. Through the breathing, the rhythm, the turning inward of yoga—through the *not* turning to an external thing like whacking a tennis ball or working a little bit longer—I found my first peace in long memory.

I kept going back to class, initially just for the Savasana.

Connecting to the body

YOGA, AS IT has been popularized in the west, is often practiced with pumping music. People move fast and sweat and detox. It's good exercise for the body and mind. But that wasn't the kind of yoga I encountered that Friday evening. Daniel's practice was deeply mindful—it made me take notice of things that had never before occurred to me. It was a practice that made me say, "Hmm…I can't feel my feet. If I can't feel my own feet, the connection from my brain to my feet isn't working. If the connection between my feet and brain does not work, how am I going to connect to other people?"

Before I found yoga, I couldn't feel my feet or even spread my toes—they were just down there somewhere. Nor did I know where my organs were in my belly. My insides were like a black hole between my ribcage and my knees. Can you feel where your liver is, unless it is in pain?

After a while, I found that I could lift my arches and run an energetic current up my shins and thighs and ass and heart and right out the top of my head and back down again. The power I used in previous forms of athletics to release energy was something that could be channeled and leveraged inside of the body, to heal it and balance it, and restore equilibrium and clarity to my whole organism.

The yoga practice that was handed to me started a new kind of self-inquiry: Am I aware of my breath? Where am I looking? Where are my feet? Are all four corners of my feet on the ground? Are my arches lifted away? Where are my fingers? Are they evenly aligned or evenly spaced? Am I standing tall or leaning forwards or backwards? Where am I in space? How good is my proprioception: the receiving (*receptoris*) of one's self (*proprius*)? Am I aware of my own body's parts in relationship to each other, to the floor, to the vertical line? What am I actually feeling? What is actually happening? It was a straight line to hyperawareness.

I began to learn that the body has rising and falling energies, that when it gets certain inputs it releases certain chemicals, that there is a virtuous loop between the actions of the body and the chemicals that are released, and that this cycle is autonomic until we intervene and override it. We can start to use our breathing and our thoughts to restructure which chemicals are getting released from our minds and into our bodies. We can reprogram ourselves, literally. I didn't know what this meant until I found yoga.

Once I began, it was rapid-fire study. I went to my first class, and never looked back. That tiny studio, with a purple *Om* symbol painted on the wall, above a pizza parlor in the middle of Chicago, curtains blowing in, sirens and car horns below, became a holy place. It was there that I discovered a sense of having a permeable body: my skin was always interacting with the environment, and I was always connected. I was made of the same stuff as everything else in the universe. Eventually, I felt a physical connection to divine source on that sweaty little mat, something I never quite got in any traditional church.

I wanted to go deeper. In late 2001, right after 9/11, I went on a retreat led by power yoga founder Baron Baptiste. His easygoing introduction to yoga philosophy, musical open laugh, softness, strength, humor and accessibility just made me happy. Baron's yoga was hard—a demanding fast flow, coupled with long holds in deep postures, like 20 minutes in a hip opener known as frog. Somatic theory says we hold our painful memories in the body, and 20 minutes in frog had women in the room letting go and weeping at all the things held in the groin and hips.

I took his teacher training in Tulum, just to keep learning or growing. Then I stumbled, or was led, into a month of teacher training in an intense, academic program with Yogarupa Rod Stryker—who honored a deep Indian lineage and knowledge base. That training has continued apace for the last 15 years , from the yoga of sound, to contact yoga, breathwork, Sanskrit- it's an unending investigation. But mostly it's a living experiment into how to have the happiest and most authentic experience in a human body. Yoga, like certain forms of martial arts and dance, is about a full range of motion. It focuses on energetics (the controlled movement and manipulation of energy through the body) and not just muscle and bone. Yoga has intention; it is used primarily to cultivate an internal awareness and connection with the body, to change our state of being.

Other sports and forms of exercise also do this to a degree, but their primary focus is external: What is the ball doing? What is the competitor doing? What is the mountain doing? What are my tools or equipment doing? In walking or running or biking, the movements can be mindful, but they are also linear. Many joints and directionalities in the body go unexplored.

In yoga, dance and martial arts, however, there is complete joint exploration, bending and moving in every way a body can bend and move. These cultivate strength, suppleness, comfort in strange or unfamiliar positions, resilience, and more. I'm not single minded: I still dance every week. Sometimes I do basic Aikido. But for me, nothing compares to yoga, in which the only tools needed are the body and breath.

Who is thinking these thoughts?

By investigating the body, I began to investigate the mind also, and then even deeper into relationships.

Once, early on, I was holding a yoga position called side plank for a long time. This position requires the body to form a long, firm, extended board, placing one hand on the floor, the other to the ceiling, and balancing between the side of the bottom foot and the palm of the hand, holding the belly snug and the hips high. It can be rigorous. My arms started shaking; my balance was challenged.

At that moment the teacher said, "People... you've held this position for a long time. I invite you to look at your reaction to that. Are you gritting your teeth and tensing your jaw and toughing it out, even though you're beyond your capacity? Are you collapsing and quitting because your conditioned mind is telling you it's too hard, even though you probably could stay longer if you wanted to? Are you feeling proud, or maybe the inverse: inadequate?"

"However you are meeting this posture on the mat," he continued, "I guarantee you: That's how you are meeting your life *off* the mat. How can you be kind to yourself in this moment, play your edge, and take responsibility for your experience? How much are your own thoughts and reactions responsible for your own suffering?"

How much? Maybe one hundred percent.

If side plank was hard, the other big practice, seated meditation, was harder. Sitting still, harboring a quiet mind, initially felt impossible. Even two minutes of meditation felt interminable. Every part of me resisted. It felt unproductive, and wasn't burning calories. To make it easier, all kinds of techniques were offered: Watch your breath right where it enters and exits the nostrils, imagine a flame, say a mantra. But it was all just practice to do one thing: to notice the workings of the mind, and to let thoughts just pass by. To become a watcher of my own thoughts.

But if I am *watching* my thoughts, who is *thinking* the thoughts? If I am witnessing them, they can't be the essence of me. These thoughts must be separately constructed. HEY! I am not my thoughts. And if I am not my thoughts, I can un-identify and manipulate them to a better outcome. Lo and behold, this was true. By watching and stopping unhelpful patterns of thinking, I learned that I could change the day-to-day experience of life in my body.

I still haven't met a single person who has been able to overcome really bad wiring without some kind of meditation practice. Well, maybe one person.

For example, I learned not to judge a rising emotion or thought, but to see it as neutral energy. If all thoughts and actions are only energy, neither positive nor negative, I can transmute it. I can remove the negative element, and just use the energy. If an unsettling or disturbing thought would arise, I would ask myself, *what can I do other than sit here or numb out through work or busyness or sex or distraction? What can I do to not numb out, to really feel and then leverage the emotion? Can I channel it into awareness, creative force, or even just let it pass through me?*

Most of the productivity and creativity in my life has been the result of having learned to transmute whatever intense emotion is coming up into an activity or action that is in touch with experience, rather than pushing it away.

Now, if I have distrubing thoughts, I can choose to be matter of fact: "Here it what it means to be in a human body; these are some of the liabilities/ Or, "I've been here before, it will pass." I can realize "Oh, that's just misperception talking, that's not my highest self."

With yoga, the recovery time from these disturbances, delusions and illusions and suffering is shorter. It takes hardly any time anymore to come back, maybe a minute or two of breathing and, whoomp—there it is! This is especially useful in navigating the daily kind of potential offenses in traffic or in the supermarket parking lot—*is this my best self acting here? Or something else?*

Meditation practice is a key tool for acquiring the emotional skills and intelligence to self-regulate, especially needed if we didn't learn it naturally in our early lives. The ability to control one's own mind and manage the fluctuations of one's emotions was key to making shifts in my life, to optimizing problem-solving and driving creative insight. When I started meditating, everything in my life, the great things and the ugly things, were all right there staring at me. I got to make the decisions: (1) that I was going to recognize when something was not right; and (2) that I would act on these realizations. Moreover, by accessing my own inmost nature, I arrived at a place where I could begin to connect with other people at the point of *their* inmost nature.

The yogic ideal is strength and suppleness, being rooted yet able to reach, the perfect combination of grounded and flexible. There is an Indian fable that puts it sweetly: the serpent Ananta, an incarnation of a deity, is coiled up. Resting on his coils is the lord Vishnu—while on the top of Ananta's head, the Earth is balanced. Ananta is strong enough to support the world, yet soft enough to be a couch for the gods.

That's what I aspired to be. Strong like that, and equally soft. I started going to class to feel better, and fell in love with the practice, and it gave me back my life. All of these tools rooted me in a life-giving and life-affirming mindset, rather than the old soup of pervasive inadequacy. Yoga made me strong, mentally and physically. But the mind can still be a storm. It creates fluctuations, and we suffer because we associate our true self with these fluctuations.

If my practice lapses, the old "stuff" is still there—those rusty circuits hardwired after my mother's murder, my father's silence and rages; raising four children of my own and then two borrowed; decades of competitive striving that seemed at the time to never be adequate—you know, those habits are happy to come back and reassert their dominance! Minding your mind is like building any muscle.

It hasn't always been comfortable for me to change, to practice this much and over this much time. But I have to practice in the face of doubt. I have to summon a warrior consciousness, to have the strength and fortitude and enthusiasm (from *en-theos*, or "feeling god from within" or "with god") to show up on the mat when my mind is telling me to lie down and read a novel instead.

With age, I am starting to see that my body is changing, and my face is changing. There has been a lot of passing of older people around me. I've watched my grandmother and asked myself, *how do you go from middle-aged to 100, should you be so lucky, with grace and elegance and without loss of power?* I'm looking into the faces of people who've lived well and fully—people who did not, at the end of their lives, wonder "Is this all there is?", but who knew that *all is*, and all will always be.

This dance of asana (the postures) and breath has been a pretty good roadmap for living. Through it, I have glimpsed self-love and respect for innate wisdom. I have learned about not being tossed around by others, by the culture, by external expectations. And I've learned that spirituality is not withdrawing into a cave, but rather living with deeper ethics in self, community, and planet care, of less consumption and more relationship. It's getting *more* connected to life in the body, not less. I have even discovered an umbilical cord to source (some people call it the divine, god, energy, love, the creative impulse—the unifying force that runs through all manifest things in the universe), unmediated by preachers, scriptures, or hierarchies.

Do you know that saying "Lift while you climb"? That translates into bringing others along with you. Whatever you know, you are obligated to pass on: Those who know must teach. If you know, you owe. In everyday life, anxiety (and all the forms of muffling that anxiety, from drugs to shopping) creates much unneeded suffering. There is so much unmet need for easefulness. I wanted everyone to feel what was possible. So, I started teaching.

Teaching yoga, helping one person at a time find the tools and technologies to achieve the Poise of the Soul, is a great gift. I sometimes teach Vinyasa flow classes. Sometimes, I teach extremely stiff people, and witness what it means to grow old without being connected to your body—it is not for the faint of heart. But I also see the relief they get from a single new insight or opening into a joint or the breath. It makes me recall my very first practice, and remember each time a teacher gave me a new posture or an insight. It reawakens gratitude and it gifts me with joyful learning. The teaching and the learning are cyclical, and the look on people's faces as they come out of Savasana is like Christmas morning for me, every time.

The science of breath

THERE IS SCIENCE behind yoga, of course. The breath, in and of itself, is an amazing access point to our entire physical and psychological selves. On the whole, our breathing is automatic: the brainstem controls the rate of breathing in response to blood-oxygen levels, as measured by receptors in the aorta. These blood-oxygen levels change in response to demands made by other systems in the body. For example, if you burst into a run, the demand for blood oxygen immediately increases, causing you to breathe faster.

"High alert" moments cause the amygdala, a part of the brain involved in experiencing emotions and governing survival instincts, to emit a message to the body: the sympathetic nervous system is activated. Breathing speeds up, the heart beats faster, blood flow is diverted from things like digestion and other secondary systems such as cell repair and into the muscles, just in case a "fight or flight" moment is coming. If the high alert continues, the limbic system adds more fuel: Adrenaline and cortisol, what we call the stress hormones, are dumped into the bloodstream. These are okay in the short term; in fact, they are necessary in the face of danger. But if stress hormones are elevated for an extended period, we have a problem. Chronic stressors take energy away from long-term system health; this is where we see conditions such as heart disease, cancer, stroke and diabetes. They also change the way the brain functions, and decrease the capacity to "stand-down" in the face of perceived stressors. If we are on high alert, in defensive mode, we can't connect—not to ourselves or to anyone else.

But while breath is *usually* automatic, it's not exclusively so. Respiration is the only part of the Autonomic Nervous System over which we have control, and breath work (the voluntary control of the breath) is the tool by which we can gain this control. Once we have it, we can use regulated breathing to override conditioned responses to perceived threats. In turn, we can regulate heart rate, blood pressure, digestion, excretion and absorption, and the release of stress hormones into the body. We can, in effect, alter the brain's information processing, making an intervention that improves our psychological functioning.

I kept going back to class, just for Savasana. If I was lethargic or down and needed a jolt of caffeine, I learned that rapid inhaling through the top of the nose and fluttering of the solar plexus and abdominal muscles would hyper-oxygenate my brain. That released a set of chemicals that told my body that I was in need of alertness and attention, reminding me to wake up and focus. While doing long, slow, even breathing, I learned that my body felt safe. This breathing also sent my nervous system a message: "I am not in threat, and I will readjust the chemicals that are now being distributed through this body."

The Yoga of Sound:
Harmonic tools

IN ADDITION TO the breathing, postures, concepts and meditations, there's another toolset that's available: the yoga of sound, vibration, and mantra. The "yoga of voice." We become comfortable with and start to cultivate our voices, the very timbre and range of them, and eventually even our words.

A lot of people sing—for fun, in the shower, in the car. And a lot of people don't. They keep their voices clenched and closed. They hold back their enthusiasm and words and the truth of their being. Those who do sing in a structured way—in a church choir or an a cappella group—know that it takes a lot of time and practice. A person has to show up in order to perform.

Doing a chant in a yoga studio is a different kind of singing. There is no audience. It is for yourself. It is for spirit. In the yoga of voice, we learn to let sound open the musculature and resonate, sending vibrations throughout the body. We use the expansion of the lungs to get into corners no stretching will ever reach. Singing teaches us to stretch from the inside: the breath fills the lungs to capacity and moves the ribs and the spine and stretches the muscles, like the stretching you would do before a run.

There is a precursor to our singing voices. We start with really deep breathing, and then by making "Om" sounds. Then we move the sound from our base all the way up through our chests, into our heads and out of our mouths. We use sound to vibrate the inner chambers of our bodies.

See what it feels like to spread that sound through your whole body. How big can it get? What is its range and tone and color? When your chest and heart are open, when your sinuses are open, when you are dropped in and unlocked, you find your own true sound. You may, for the first time, find the actual sound of your own voice!

I've heard big men with wispy voices drop into profound resonant warm speaking tones when the chest and breath are expanded. As I have discovered my own voice, I have begun to form my words in a way that is real and authentic, too. Our voices are an extension of our bodies and an extension of our heads and mind, and there are parallels between finding the tone and the content of the voice and the content of what we have to say. The more sounds we make and the greater the range of the sounds we make, the more fully these sounds reflect the bundle of ideas we have inside.

The most beautiful thing about the yoga voice is simply making sounds: *Hum, Om, Ram, Lam.* These sounds are pure expression, without words. When practiced with a group, there is no interpretation; and there is no misinterpretation. We are just here. Each person's own sound comes out. We are simply vibrating, and the emotion in that is of connecting and listening to ourselves and to others without trying to ascribe meaning.

When was the last time you vocalized for no reason? How low or how high, how wide, how big or how small, how whiny, how many different kinds of sounds can you make? When no one is looking, what tone do you settle in at? How does your voice change if you are in a shitty mood or stressed? Can you feel an interesting reflection of what is going on inside you, with your disposition in the moment?

When you do these sounds with a group, in a call and response format, the leader sings a line of a mantra, and the community repeats it back. The energy transfer between yoga call and response is tight. Whatever energy is inside those leading and those following in the rows, whatever people are coping with, it passes through each person in the group and is absorbed.

Sometimes the same phrase is repeated over and over for 20 minutes or more, adding different instrumentation and different rhythm, faster and faster, then slowing it down. There's so much power in the singing, that the sound coming from each person combines into one body of sound. The group becomes an organism—inhaling, exhaling, inhaling until the entire group has been unified by sound.

The yoga of voice, of chant, has nothing to do with performance, and everything to do with creating a unified voice. It's a conscious choice to JOIN with each other. And that is where I want to be in the present moment: within a community seeking to create a conscious organism together. Author Jeff Greenwald said, "It's impossible to feel lonely when you're singing."

I now sing my prayers in the morning with my harmonium by myself and that is for nobody—it's just devotion. When I do sing with people, it's to be connected to others who are in a state of surrender. I can open up really big, and draw out a lot of emotion; this expression invites other people to dig deep, open up, sing their hearts out and let go, too.

COMING FULL CIRCLE

Lovers and fighters

DURING MY FIRST five years of teaching, the students were 90 percent white women, practicing in beautiful calm spaces with bamboo flooring and dim lighting and burning sage. When the women entered the studio, they generally sat down quietly, not talking to anybody, and prepared to go inward and pay attention to their bodies. Even though many took the practice seriously, I was mainly attracting people who wanted a yoga butt and great triceps, and of course, who had the money for classes.

I wanted to reach more and different kinds of people with yoga, so I sought out other places to teach. I'd get out of the ghetto of privilege and see who was out there. I'd already begun to work on peace initiatives with the international yoga community, which worked to put yoga and mindfulness teachers in war zones and on military bases worldwide, but thought doing it hands-on would be less abstracted, more connecting.

In a strip mall a few blocks away from my luxurious yoga studio, there was a Mexican fighting gym. My fiercely beautiful friend Vic was the head trainer. These two communities—yoga and fighting—don't talk to each other at all. After some conversation and generous flirtation, Vic suggested that I offer classes to his guys.

Heeding the directive that there is an obligation to teach when you are called. I was a full yes for teaching anywhere. But in this case, there was another motivator at work as well: curiosity about what that place was like, and what those people were like. In the interest of being a bridge, I took him up on his offer. I started to going over twice a week to offer classes to his fighters.

There was a long, winding countertop where you checked in. They sold extreme sports drinks, protein powders, products that jack you up. The room was wide open, with bright colors and bright lights. In the middle was a boxing ring. On the ground was a cushy floor of mats for practicing flip throws, and around the periphery of the room was weight training equipment. At any given time, 30 to 40 people would be in various stages of training while Top 40 songs or hip hop or rap blared in the background. It was an environment designed for the practice of whacking each other in the head. Not a single, traditional mindfulness object—no Buddha heads or candles or lotus blossoms or chant bowls or goddess statues—existed in the entire space.

When we started "yoga time" we had to quiet the room. Victor had everybody in the gym stop weight training and come out of the ring to join this part of the class. We did warm ups, joint conditioning, breath work and postures tailored to improve misalignments in their bodies, but there wasn't much flowing silent vinyasa.

Here are a few things I noticed in the first minutes of class: The men refused to take off their socks; they could not be quiet for a second; they were punching each other in the shoulders; they were checking each other out the whole time. There was this incredible masculine energy and macho culture. To walk into a teaching situation like that, so boisterous, where the guys are overtly making jokes at each other about the adequacy of their various body parts—how was I supposed to enter into that culture and say, "Hey, brothers, we're going to get quiet and listen to our breath. We're going to take off our socks even if we don't like what our feet look like, because our feet are the basis of how we move; everything comes from how our feet touch the ground, and energy ripples up from there. So let's get intimate with our feet."

There were all kinds of seemingly minute obstacles that I hadn't imagined could be issues in teaching. For example, the guys were wearing nylon shorts; if they turned upside down, they had naked legs up to the groin. My ladies at the studio had the right clothes, so going upside down wasn't a peep show. Moreover, this yoga thing had not been initiated by the men, but by their teacher. Initially, maybe three of the 35 men in that class could stop posturing for their peers and participate in the exercise of turning their attention inward.

I also didn't know how to be in conversation. I was in a room full of athletes who were really good at what they did, but they didn't know the anatomical names of their body parts. So "descending the scapula" or "engaging the quadriceps" meant nothing to them. I left each class with a quiet, meditative inquiry: *Please guide me to know how best to teach to these guys.*

And it came.

There is some part of me that's a teenaged boy. I thought of what worked to reach or talk to my own boys. Rather than impose what I thought of as yoga on them, I upped my energy and joined them in their boisterousness. I didn't ask them to stop talking or do a lot of the things you would do if you were leading a class. I met them where they were. In letting them be where they were, and then working with those individuals who were paying attention and interested, our work together started to turn.

One guy, Jorge, was about twenty. He was slim and agile and a talented fighter. He had extreme closure on his chest; he was collapsed in the collarbones, really protected. As a result, there was a lot of pressure on his upper back and neck. I started working with him to bring his shoulder blades down and get his head balanced over his spine while moving. When I physically touched him a juvenile, sitting-in-a-tree, *OOOOOOHH* sound went up in the group.

"Look," I told them, "at his structure and his body. If this happens in a person, it produces a weakness in the spine, right *here...*" I poked. "That makes him vulnerable to injury, *and it takes away from his power.*"

Then they really looked. It was inviting them in, to look and conclude, that changed things. When they shifted into a place of examining and inquiring about each other, I began to see what moved them.

I think fighters have a natural fight in them, a natural hunger and ambition. To fight you're already learning to stay in balance, to move from the center. These men took to yoga really well. The more I could make a direct connection between what was happening in the pre-training yoga and what might happen in the ring, the more they gave their respect and attention to the practice.

This "connection first" principle can be extrapolated to other interactions. How do we make something we're sharing matter to other people? First, we have to know what job they're trying to get done. What matters to them? Where are they finding difficulty or pain or training or the mental game that might be lagging, and how can what offer help?

An example of this mentality from my work with the fighters is the way we worked on marrying breath to movement. In yoga, when you bend forward you exhale, and when you arc backward you're inhaling. The movement serves the breath. This breathing puts more power in every movement. By demonstrating how to align breath with movement—and what the result could be—the fighters I worked with learned another tool that they could take into the ring, or use anywhere.

We began using the breath to calm anxiety. "Hey, your opponent is coming at you, and you use this breathing technique to bring your nervous system into alignment." Eventually this transformed into, "Just because your girlfriend's mad at you, you don't have to react. You can use this same breathing technique." We began to talk about how to listen to the body for clues; how, if you're suddenly tense and don't know why, you can get quiet and listen to what your body is telling you.

Within ten weeks of starting our sessions, their form was excellent. They were breathing deeply with the movements, making new jokes reminding each other to get still: "Hey, man! You can't hear your own breath when you're talking!"

There was a transformation. They began to take yoga seriously, and they translated this into learning about their bodies, feeling more transparent and having more power and ease and freedom. They started to treat yoga as part of their regular training.

As a teacher, I'd had to get through my own cultural misunderstandings. I, too, was transformed. Frankly, I didn't want to go back to teach the "old way" after I'd worked with the fighters. I preferred teaching people who didn't necessarily have the yoga costume and ritual, but were just open.

The heart of being known, is knowing each other's story. I can dance around the edges and tell an approximation of other people's truths, but only they can tell their full story. I could ask them questions and probe, so that they could tell a more authentic and richer version of their truth, but I couldn't make up stuff about them and wish it to be true. In their movements and in the dialogues, they were telling me the truth of their stories, and in their own way. We were having a conversation.

Why don't people do this kind of bridge-building more often? This problem isn't just in the neighborhood, between boys and women or Mexicans and Anglos or fighters and yogis—this separation is everywhere. Recently I was at a client's company, a Fortune 500 company. In the lunchroom, just like in high school, the tables were segregated: the blacks, the Japanese natives, the white clerical workers. Why is there this disconnect? Why aren't we talking with each other?

It is, of course, a two-way street. If the counterparty doesn't want to connect and there's no port to plug into, it can feel like you're banging your head against the wall. The guy who owned the gym wanted to have some co-ed yoga practice, but the girls didn't want to do it with the boys. They didn't want to put their butts in the air in front of the men. So we practiced in a back room. These four girls wore bubble gum lip polish and flipped their hair; they were sassy and proud of their strength—but I had never worked with anyone who was tougher to reach than those girls. Though we were in a back room there were glass windows on the room, so people could see in; maybe that produced some discomfort. We also didn't have enough time to build trust. To be a girl who fights, I think you've got to go through some tough things. Your armor has got to be up. They wouldn't meet me, or I wasn't skilled at meeting them. With more time, maybe, maybe we could have gotten there. But the point was in the trying. Even though I couldn't make the connection I wanted, I set out with an attitude of love and let our work be what it was.

As each of us is a unique expression of the creative force, I'm actively looking for that place of magic in another. I could walk into that Mexican fighting gym and say to those men and those young girls, "I don't know you." But my assumption about them needed to be this: *"There is something completely unique and valuable about you, and I cannot wait to find out what it is."*

To be able to categorize people, to have a way that all things fit together, can feel comfortable and easy. To walk in a world where judgment and prejudice are common, and to try to drop those habits—that can be hard. Inquiry and being present to people's expression and inner work and reality takes time, but it is so worth it.

In Vic's gym, some of that rage and sorrow that came along with my mother's milk, was washed away. Wherever I could, I extended my personal healing practices to others. The men in the fighting gym were only a beginning. More and more, I felt guided to be in conversation with complete strangers.

Consciously or not, I had leapt into a swift river that was quickly going to carry me into some increasingly strange corners.

Rusty says, "I'm sorry"

AROUND THE SAME time as the fighting gym experience, I saw a flyer for James Fox's "yoga in prisons" program. I signed up for the training immediately.

The orientation was held in a large, sunlit yoga studio in Berkeley, CA. Mirrors lined one full wall, reflecting the light coming in through high windows. The floors were hardwood. Everything was very clean. I entered the room and joined the other teaching candidates already sitting in a circle.

Sitting next to me in that circle was Jacques Verduin, a handsome Dutch Buddhist with a full mop of salt and pepper hair. Jacques had founded Insight Out, an overarching program that includes as one of its branches, a yoga in prison program. He coordinates a program at San Quentin called GRIP, or Guiding Rage Into Power, educating life-eligible inmates toward self-awareness and away from violence.

At the head of the circle sat a man. He stood up, and walked to the front of the room.

"Hi, I'm Rusty," he said, calmly and with poise. "In the summer of 1977, I killed a woman. I served 32 years in San Quentin Prison, where I met Jacques and began doing this work. Now I am paroled and working in the community—the very community that I came out of. I'm working with young men like me, to help stop them from taking the path I did, to teach them new skills.

"The first thing I'd like to do is to apologize personally to each and every one of you who has been the victim of a crime."

He paused and sat back in his chair in the circle. His gaze traveled around the room; he made eye contact with each person, bowing to them and acknowledging their place in this circle.

In that moment everything popped into place. I didn't show up at training that day to be a healer; I was there to be healed.

When Rusty looked at me, tears started streaming down my face. My mother had been killed during the same summer that Rusty had committed his crime. Rusty's apology was the first I had ever received. I had been waiting decades to hear those words from someone, and I didn't even know it. The apology went straight into my heart, tapping into a well of unfelt sorrow that I didn't even know was there.

When James asked the teacher candidates in the room to introduce ourselves, I spoke about my mother's murder. I told them what that apology meant to me. I told them that I was sure that I was meant to be in that room, on that day. And I told Rusty that I was grateful to him. His willingness to do the work, and how he showed up on that day, had given me the hope of transformation, evidence that someone can shift.

Jacques Verduin's project, I'd learn, works. GRIP delivers results for victims, offenders, prisons, communities, and taxpayers in a repeatable, scalable, low cost way.

In addition to Yoga, or somatic healing, one element of the GRIP program is victim-offender communication and reconciliation. As the light faded on my first day of training, Jacques stopped me on the way out the door. "Do you think," he asked, "that you would be able to come to the prison and talk to the men about what it was like for you as a child to lose your mother to murder? About the long shadow of violence? About your own anger work? Will you stand in for their victim and be in dialogue with them as their victim?"

I gulped hard. The knowledge that Rusty had shifted so much, that he had changed in his core, that that was even possible, was powerful. In my pursuit to live in love and inquiry, meeting people who had committed murder and were working through that in their own lives seemed to be a milestone.

But could I do this? Could I sit in a room of people who were so far gone that they had killed another human being, and be in dialogue? Three weeks after meeting Jacques, I went with him to visit the GRIP classroom at San Quentin.

Change in extremis:
A prison bodhisattva

S AN QUENTIN IS perched on the shoreline of the San Francisco Bay and at the foot of the Richmond Bridge, with a gorgeous waterfront, moist ocean air, and a view of Marin's Mt. Tamalpais in the distance. The prison was built in 1855 and has the look of a castle, a crenellated hulk with gothic arched windows. The whole place, other than the building blocks themselves, feels totally antiquated. Every process is paper-based: you sign in and out on clipboards. Paper laminate IDs peel at the corners, signs are washed out, there is dirt in the corners, mismatched furniture, cracked cement, chain link fences leaning every which way.

On the appointed day, I signed in at the gate. The guards took my ID and held it. We signed in again at the main entrance to the building. It was busy. People of all stripes—medical personnel, priests, guards, volunteers, employees—went in and out like they were going through a subway turnstile. Jacques and I passed through a double holding space, where a floor-to-ceiling metal grate closed behind us. Once that had closed, another opened to let us into the prison.

Inside there is a gesture toward landscaping. On that blue-sky, late-fall day, garden flowers in primary colors shouted against the neutral cement backdrop. There are signs on buildings and painted lines on sidewalks all saying "out of bounds" to indicate where a prisoner can and can't go. There is a post office and a hobby shop, where prisoners sell what they have made. There are chapels, and a church, directly across from death row. There are a few trailers and low-lying buildings where rooms are used for continuing education and therapy sessions. All of these rooms are multipurpose, and

73

everything is heaped on top of everything else in ramshackle piles. There is a hospital. Jacques told me the hospital was built on an executive order from three Federal judges, because too many people were dying in prison due to lack of medical care. Jacques and I crossed through the yard and to one of the education buildings.

I'd been told no jeans, no blue shirts, no neon. Now it was evident why: the men were all in blue jeans or blue shirts or blue, prison-issue pants that look like hospital gear. The prisoners being transported were in neon jumpsuits. The guys in the yard were wearing white gym shorts.

As we approached another guard shack, a correctional officer yelled out, "Who are you?"

I'd had a feeling, from the strict instructions I'd been given, that I was and would be treated as an outsider. This guard confirmed that notion. While most of the nurses and teachers and visitors seemed to be women, it was clear to me that they didn't like women walking around the prison. I was wearing black, straight leg jeans and the guard said they were too revealing, and I'd have to wear scrubs over them. I'm not an immodest dresser; I could tell that no matter what I was wearing, there'd be a problem. Part of this is safety, but most of it seemed to be about power and control. Immediately, I felt their judgment. There is a tradition of disdain in the dynamic between guards and outsiders: classes for prisoners run by outsiders, for example, are derisively called "Hug-a-thug" programs.

I stuck close to Jacques, who remained calm and composed at every obstacle.

I was not afraid, just self-conscious. I don't know what I was expecting, but here is what I wasn't expecting: doubles tennis in full swing. Half-court basketball in full swing. And in the education building itself? The classrooms had those little alphabet strips, the first-grade writing charts with the double lines and dashes and the arrows showing which way to make a letter, teaching grown men how to read and write in cursive. There was shelf holding *A History of the United States*, the same textbook my kids had used in eighth grade.

We signed in at another entry point and went into the classroom itself, moving tables away and circling up the chairs. There were no guards in this room.

The men came in and took seats around the circle. R: Red beard, maybe a size 14 shoe. T: Maybe Filipino; he hardly spoke. R2: Lanky, 6'4 at least; a big blue long-distance stare. R3: A charismatic, wiry Native American. M: A handsome baby-faced black man with glasses. R4: Asian, middle aged; he kept falling asleep. F: A young Mexican man with small hands, a compact body. Each of these men would serve in San Quentin for 20 or 30 years—they were all long term prisoners, and life eligible inmates. There are 34,000 of them in California alone.

Then there was me, and Jacques.

These men—who at some point have killed— are engaged in a year-long program to become non-violent persons and peacemakers. They have taken a student peacekeeper pledge, I learned—a pledge that people 'from the outside' can also partake in.

Jacques left the room, and I tried some small talk. "This is the first time I've been in a prison," I said.

To which Robin replied, "What kind of prison? There are all kinds—like the one in your head."

"Or an abusive relationship," Robert chimed in. "That's a prison. Or a financial prison."

So this is how it's gonna be, I thought. No small talk. Right to the big stuff.

When Jacques returned, he asked me to tell my story. I tried to lead with the facts, and not with my reaction. I tried to recreate what happened on the night of my mother's murder from what I had pieced together from the police reports.

At this point, I knew that she had been killed on June 20, and found on July 3.

"My mother's body was found in a cornfield off the interstate, near Zionsville, Indiana," I told them. "The current Sheriff of Boone County was just a new patrolman on duty then. He said she had been severely abused, and that she had been stabbed. A lot of bad things. That is what I know. She was identified by her dental records," I told them.

"She was on her way to see a photo stylist; she was working for a women's magazine, and was going to do a shoot in Indianapolis. I think that is the story," I paused.

I cannot remember the act of telling the story that day. I felt detached from my body. It was too hard for me to connect with the depth of my own emotions, so I numbed out instead.

"I was 11 years old, and suddenly my source of warmth and comfort and assurance was ripped away. It changed everything for me in an instant."

I talked about how I watched my father cry for the first time, how I've felt my mother's absence at every major milestone in my life. I talked about my anger and bewilderment around raising my own children, on having to learn that from someone else. I delivered the facts without emotion. "There isn't a day that goes by," I said, " that some shadow of that event doesn't show up."

In my delivery, I was flatlining—feeling nothing—and then I cracked. There was no attempt at composure.

When Jacques asked for reactions, one man choked up. He said, "The man I killed had a baby son. That boy will never know his father, and your story reminds me of that."

A large part of going into San Quentin and doing the victim-offender work is hearing the stories of the men and being able to ask them the hardest questions victims might have.

"How can you kill a person?" I asked. "What goes through your head? How could you take a life? Why do you think what you want in the moment is more important than someone else's life? How could someone have looked at my beautiful, vibrant mother and thought that they would end her life? Did they ever wonder who else it would impact?"

There was a long pause. Then, one by one, with strong self-awareness and clarity, they told their stories.

At 17, 18, 19, 20, each ended up in a scenario where they chose to take a life. A common theme was this: these men, as children, knew nothing of what it meant to be loved and held and safe. From an early age they knew nothing but drugs and violence. They spoke of abusive foster care, running interference on drug deals and domestic discord, a sense of being isolated, of being judged, of being on their own, of building daily defenses against closeness. The abuse they received was their schooling on how to treat others.

Another thread was this: they often did what they did out of a misplaced longing for love and acceptance. One man said as much. It mattered more to him, on the streets at 17 and in that moment he killed, to be accepted by the other two boys he was with, to be one of the gang, than to consider the life of the man he murdered. His act of turning away from the family that abused him—and turning toward the street for a new family—was an attempt to find the love he did not get from his mother. Or, out of loyalty: Many killed in defense of a loved one.

Every story contained a five-second (or at most a one-minute), impulsive decision. Conditions were created in which the men went over the edge: one blow, one wrong step. Then it was done; no amount of regret could bring the victim back.

I felt, literally, that if there had been a small shift in trajectory, I could have been them. There was so much confusion and movement and abandonment and reaching out for love when I was young. Had I not had some degree of privilege, and some love anchoring from a few members of my family and a particularly wonderful high school teacher, it could have been me on the street.

When young people spend their lives seeking love, it's not uncommon for them to make unwise decisions that will affect their entire lives. Once we do something we are ashamed of, or that we can't take back, we can't rewind the clock. It begins to define us, and lives with us all the time.

I related to their stories. Trying to go on in the face of being shunned, and trying to manage my anger but not having the tools. And I related to them as people. My heart was breaking for each of them, for the children they had been. Their own victimization had pre-destined them to victimize in return. They'd had no chance at all. The anger I felt at the world for my own losses and perceived slights? It was the same anger they had; I had just acquired more coping skills along the way. And I'd had my grandparents and their grounding force. Through parenting and yoga and walking in nature, I had been able to channel my rage and anger, transform it into positive energy. But these men hadn't gotten to that point before they committed the crime that landed them in San Quentin. Still, we were more alike than I ever would have imagined.

Restorative justice

I WONDERED WHY my understanding of what contributed to crime, and the reality of imprisonment in the United States was so limited. So I dug into the data.

As an advocate for victims' rights, my mind was fundamentally changed. Prisons are rooted in disconnection, designed to isolate and remove people from both society and each another. We remove people who we think are a danger to mainstream society to "do their time," and then we return them to society; but they still bear the legacy of being excluded, and they are not only unhealed, but often they are more dangerous.

Prison has a lot of justice-oriented goals: to punish those who have harmed others or society (punitive); to lock up unsafe people and keep them off the streets (defensive); and to re-train and restore people who have acted against the law to a healthy role in society (rehabilitative). Sentencing is notoriously unjust and vague, and is sometimes applied arbitrarily based on race, jurisdiction and the mood of the judge. The highest and best use of a prison—to put people into a secure container where they can learn new behaviors, change patterns and then return to society safer—is seldom achieved.

Prisons are packed with men holding memories of their own crimes, and years of rejection from mainstream society. There is an endless dance of control and violence in word, thought and deed. In many cases, when people are locked up, they get even more violent and embedded in criminal activity. More prisons are being commissioned away from communities (where volunteer organizations can serve them effectively) and built in remote areas in the name of "job creation," making the aims of a restorative justice program even more difficult to achieve.

But there are people working inside of these systems to make restoring the capability for measured response and reconnection the primary goal of incarceration. Through this example, I have witnessed inmates' shifting trajectory in real time. They are finding ways to understand the impacts of their actions, ways to develop and continue building emotional intelligence. They are doing deep inner work, learning ways to shift their behavior, to interrupt violent impulses in order to empower and enlighten themselves, and to create and implement new practices, belief patterns, and policies.

Guiding Rage Into Power is one example of a program that is restorative instead of destructive. And it's creating connection and even joy in the most unlikely of institutions.

Here's how it's done. A belief system, with the constructs that reflect that system, is recognized and studied. Then new beliefs that better align with the greater purpose of the institution are enacted. The new beliefs break the cycle from within. Essentially, they beat the system.

One of the first things that GRIP participants are asked to do is sign a pledge. As I left, the men showed me the pledge they were making. It demanded a full year of living in awareness and learning the skills to change the way they live in the world.

The men wondered: Would I sign the pledge, too? I looked. I read it. I asked myself. Could *I* try to live like this? The pledge would be hard for most people on the outside to keep.

Inmates are expected to renounce any other affiliations they may have for the duration of the program and—if they graduate from the program—forever. That means they are no longer part of the Aryan Brotherhood or the Crips or whoever is in power on the yard. They are no longer part of that world. This is their new family; they are now part of this tribe—across all of those former affiliations and loyalties. This tribe is about healing, with each member a healing agent.

Could you sign it?

GUIDING RAGE INTO POWER:

Student's pledge on being nonviolent and being a peacemaker (© Jacques Verduin)

Taking this pledge is about transforming my violence and healing my rage, starting with me, here and now. I make this pledge as a student and if I graduate from the GRIP Program in 12 months, I will have gained the skills to turn this pledge into a life-long commitment in the presence of my community.

I pledge to:

» Stop my violence and practice peaceful ways of interacting with myself and others.

» Pray for healing for my victims and dedicate my study of this program to them.

» Learn how to respond rather than react by learning to mindfully observe my experience through regular practice so I can make wise decisions.

» Treat my physical body with care by not overworking or overdoing and finding a balance between work & rest. I will strive to eat wisely, not smoke, or use alcohol or other substances.

» Be true to my word and do as I say. I commit to being transparent and truthful because lying is abusive.

» Take only things that are given freely, not take things that don't belong to me and live within my means.

» Learn how to listen to myself and others, especially those who disagree with me.

» Understand that blaming, judging & criticizing people is disempowering and creates conflict. I strive to forgive others, let go of grudges and resentments and apologize whenever it is helpful to do so.

» Take responsibility for how I regulate my emotions, understanding that ultimately other people never make me feel the way I feel.

» Strive to learn how to express genuine affection, achieve intimacy and not harm others as a sexual being.

» Strive to establish equality in my relationships with other beings (especially women). I also strive to establish equality with people of different races, color, gender, sexual orientation, stature and religious backgrounds. This also includes elders and children, as well as not harming animals and all living things on this planet.

» Engage responsibility as an opportunity, not a burden; as a way to self-actualize and create change in the world.

» Seek to understand and communicate the needs underneath my anger or frustration. Commit to processing my feelings and find strength in my ability to be vulnerable.

» Become someone who seeks to understand more than seeks to be understood.

» Share with other program participants and not hide the times I fail to stick to this pledge.

» Challenge violence firmly but kindly, in all its forms wherever I encounter it and to stand with others who are treated unfairly, even if it means standing alone. I commit to this program as if life depends on it, because I understand that it does.

I, _____, commit myself to becoming a nonviolent person and a trained peacekeeper.

I do victim-offender communication and reconciliation sessions a few times a year. As the GRIP program runs in cycles, I am there for about three weeks of it, usually once in October or November, and once in February or March. There has never been a session as raw as the first one, but they are always powerful.

When I share my story, I try not to make it abstract. I try to say, "This is what it felt like to be 11 and to lose my mother. This is how it followed me through my whole life." Some of them can relate, or they realize a connection to the person they killed—a man, or a woman who had children.

Every time I go in, for each three-hour session, almost everybody in the room cries, 40 men and me. Everybody bawling our eyes out because we all wish we could undo the loss and pain, on both sides.

I've also led meditation techniques to the same group. Both are used to improve the way these men function in the world. But even before I arrive, these men have experienced intense training. They've learned how to recognize the moment of imminent danger, something we deal with every day in our own lives. You are about to grab a cigarette when you are trying to stop smoking; you are about to grab a drink; you are about to yell at your spouse; you are about to lose it on your kid. They've learned how to recognize that moment in themselves, and breathe. That helps them write a new story.

They learn that their blind, immediate reaction to a thing is probably wrong, so they learn how to pause and change that reaction. They learn the difference between a reaction and a response. They build a cushion between thought and action. They learn how to slow down, and sit with emotion. Instead of pushing it away, this pause-and-recognition process allows them to see what is going on not only in themselves, but in the people around them. By the time I come in they've done the heavy lifting.

Jacques has been doing this work for twenty years, and he is changing lives and changing outcomes for prisoners. Every weekday, he has chosen to spend his time in the prison. He's trained other trainers. They've produced a video series. The state of California has hired his organization to expand the work to other prisons. He is now training sheriffs, police and other prison administrators in other countries.

Over the course of several years, I learned how Jacques approaches the work of turning people from offenders into peacekeepers. He builds the tribe. The members support each other in deep awakening, eliciting peer support and accountability. There are four planks of the program: Stopping your violence, developing emotional intelligence, cultivating mindfulness, and understanding victim impact. Together, they change the mind, body, and heart for lasting change.

Those who do the work don't hurt people anymore. The general prison population in California has a 60% recidivism rate. GRIP members, once paroled, have a 0% recidivism rate (after 4 years of data on parolees). And after a year in the program, men are eligible to assist in subsequent classes, to apprentice.

One of these men was Scott. Scott had been a shot caller on the prison yard, and had been put in solitary confinement over 1,000 times. By the time

I met him, during my first visit to San Quentin, he had been working with Jacques for five years. He was tough. His body showed it; his life story was in the muscles in his jaw. He had the jumpy twitch of someone who'd spent his youth on high alert. But his eyes were liquid, alive and full of compassion. Jacques told me that men line up outside of Scott's cell now, for advice; he's become a sort of prison bodhisattva.

When it came time for the graduation ceremony from the apprentice program, we received a special request from someone who wanted to hand Scott his certificate personally. It was a Chief Deputy Warden who had been at the prison for over 30 years. As he handed Scott his diploma, the other men watched alongside the head of California State Corrections, the warden, a Senator, and a representative from the Governor's office.

"Scott," the officer said, "it's a pleasure to be handing you this instead of another lock up order. And I want to tell you that I was skeptical. I was doubtful that this program would work. But I am humbled. It's the first time I have ever really believed that true change in a man is possible. You are all doctors. You save lives."

With Scott's success and the success of others like him, the goal of restoration is fulfilled. The journeys of these inmates have come full circle— from being excluded to being invited back into society. For me, as well, it is reconciliation. Whoever killed my mom, I now realize, was suffering as these men were suffering. I want to make that assumption, because their stories are so similar, and we are all so alike. There are so many places and times in my life when I felt the same way as these men; I just didn't pull the trigger.

Some of these men sing like angels or make beautiful art or take care of each other or are drug and alcohol counselors in the prison. Their individual stories are powerful and, taken collectively, they are instructive: Can we take someone in his wholeness, and not just for the damaging things that he did? Can we forgive? Can we believe in change? Can we bring them home, and see if they can heal their own families and neighborhoods?

In doing this work, I became aware of the way we've pushed perceived undesirable people—the sick, the criminal, the elderly—into corners. And in pushing these people away—in ghettoizing them, in stereotyping them, in turning them into cartoons—we have blocked the problem from our day-today view. Society says that if you kill another person, you are never to be forgiven. But from their stories, I understood that almost every victimizer is also a victim. They still deserve our attention, love and healing.

Like a tumor, what isn't examined persists. If ignored it will just keep growing, until it destroys its host. The severing and disconnection from the undesirable elements in society or in ourselves doesn't solve anything, it just begets more of the same. Moreover, I felt in my bones that these men, as individuals, are scapegoats for our massive brokenness as a culture. We have pushed them into a box and refused to look at the culture we have built that is making them. They are the symptoms of our structural problems, made and grown collectively, not individually.

And it is not only criminals we have pushed away; we have pushed away the sick, the poor, the elderly; we have excluded anyone who doesn't paint a rosy picture of a healthy, productive society. We refuse to look at our own shadows, even while they separates, wounds, and kills in countless ways. I think this is where our biggest potential as a culture lies.

VIOLENCE: THE ULTIMATE FORM OF DISCONNECTION

Are we natural killers?

FOR A LONG time in my life, I just accepted the idea that humans were violent. I had heard it so many times, and it was certainly evident in history and in the news. But is it true, really? Are we natural killers?

I don't feel like a killer, the people in my life don't act like that. What makes us turn on each other?

Philosopher John N. Gray investigated the fine line between civility and barbarism. He looked at societies that had experienced famines, wars, natural disasters and economic collapse, and asked: What does it take before people begin to eat each other alive; to move from communitarian values to each man for himself?

Gray postulates that while mankind's factual knowledge is growing exponentially, the knowledge of how to deal with our emotions is relatively stagnant. In fact, the understanding of how to process emotions such as greed, anger, lust, sadness and fear has to be *re-learned* experientially by each subsequent generation.

One takeaway from Gray's work is that civility—the ability to emotionally self-regulate in interactions with others—is the line that separates us from barbarism. Emotional regulation is learned is through civilization and practices. We have to teach it like we teach math (or better than we teach math).

Let's stop perpetuating the notion that aggression is in our genes and our hormones, and that violence it is simply part of human nature. The world we are born into, the environments around us, and the systems we create bear collective responsibility for the biology of violence. If one is born into less than perfect circumstances, he or she has farther to go to revalue and reconnect.

But it is indeed possible, if one does the work and the practices to get there. The guys who as kids were running drugs for their parents, or who took to the streets in their search for belonging—even at this extreme they are capable of and are actually doing the work, when given the chance.

Even if our experiences have been horrifying, they still contain seeds that can be points of departure for growth. Without new practices, we may very well play out the stories written in our youth and childhood. But this is not a fate carved in stone: we rewrite and recreate our own beings daily. We are not in a fixed state at birth, at seven, at 18, at 25, or even when we are 80—we are malleable! Think of Scott. After he was released, he began to work teaching anger management and domestic violence prevention to bankers and lawyers who are unkind to their wives and children. That is major transformation. That is "giving back."

Our lives, and any amount of loneliness, alienation or violence that we've experienced, have prepared us for something. Negative seeds in us can be physically transformed. What have our "negative experiences" prepared us for? Can we begin to look at the violence, the disconnections in our lives, as a gift? Can we create a new pattern out of what already exists? Can we transform a biology of violence into a biology of connection?

By beginning inside ourselves, examining our beliefs and cultivating new practices, we develop an inner baseline of loving kindness and open availability. From there, we can create more connection to others, and then expand away from violence and alienation in the culture at large. As our worldview shifts from "we are individual self-contained units" to "we are each part of an interconnected organism and system," our behavior changes, too.

Making active choices is a practice, and practices are the most certain way to take charge of our evolution. Our world would be more harmonious if it were full of protectors, not aggressors. In order to bring that about, those of us who live in the Western world have to do some rewiring to come back into wholeness.

Another line of inquiry I wanted to pursue was how people in wartime conditions reacted to aggression. How does war create the conditions for barbarism? The predictors of genocide are all about making one group alien, about making them "the other", and then attacking.

I sought out a particularly well-respected researcher and thinker, Lt. Col David Grossman. In his book, *On Killing*, he investigates how the military trains soldiers to kill, and the human cost of this training. Grossman's work shows that the military, working hard to make men violent, tries to actively interrupt the human ability to choose peaceful evolution.

From ancient Rome to WWII, Grossman reports, most soldiers would not kill; at the moment of decision they lowered their weapons, pretended to fire, or played dead. In WWII, some 90% of soldiers did not fire their weapons. To get soldiers to engage more violently and aggressively, the military began performing conditioning experiments, such as changing a target from a bull's eye into the outline of a person, and attaching red paint-filled balloons to the target to simulate blood. By the time the Vietnam conflict, more than 90% of soldiers fired their guns. Gradually, through iterative scientific method, the military learned to train non-killers to kill when called upon.

That generation of soldiers who came back from Vietnam was much more destroyed than their predecessors, with 30% suffering from PTSD, 2/3 of which were still suffering from it 20 years later, according to the Veterans Administration. It is partly this: they were the first group of soldiers who all *shot to kill*. Psychiatrists extracted some key learnings: becoming killers placed a schism in their identities. All of our lives we are told that killing is bad; that it violates basic moral commandments; that someone who is a good person would never do that. After the military's intense training to turn them into dutiful killers, their minds couldn't hold the contradiction. There were additional contributing factors in that the reception Vietnam veterans received on returning home was negative.

Yet, even today, with many advances in preventing and caring for PTSD in the military, between 11 and 20% of veterans of Iraq and Afghanistan conflicts report PTSD on any given day.

It seems to be this way with violent offenders, also. They weren't killers at birth, but in order to survive in a culture of pervasive violence, a culture that sometimes rewards and at other times abhors it, they too became split.

Repeat: While we can condition people to be killers, *they are absolutely not killers by birth*. Grossman asks beautifully, "what if there is a force stronger then the desire to win or to kill, and that that force is the desire to live? What if

Eros always trumps Thanatos? In an Eros dominated world, the only role of violence in a person is to be a sheep dog, never a lion, never a wolf; it is only to protect."

Even with indoctrination that says you are protecting someone or something—be it land, families, or values—the killing itself still takes a toll.

Is it in our genes?

MY EXPLORATION DIDN'T stop with social science. Some people suggest that violence is truly biological, present in us from birth, a way of asserting our will and controlling our environment. Others suggest that violence is a result of environmental factors. We used to debate whether it was nature or nurture that determined who we became and how we acted; now we know it is always both.

I began to think of this using a technology metaphor: If nature is the genetic mainframe we are born into, the hardware or the operating system our bodies run, then nurture is our programming.

There is a clear and constant interaction between genes and environment, as our environment determines which genes are called on to express themselves in daily encounters, to direct our actions. We are *who we are*, but we are also *who we become*, due to this critical interplay between genetic hardwiring and our environmental programming.

What if our disconnections, alienations, and the violence we do to one another is not biological, but a flaw in our cultural programming, our "code?" If that is the case, the intersections of biology and psychology and environment that produce disconnection and violence can be retrained.

So what does the research say?

It says, in part, that yes, there appear to be specific genetic markers for violent behavior. Guang Guo at UNC Chapel Hill has identified "three genes that play a strong role in determining why some young men raised in rough neighborhoods or deprived families become violent criminals, while others do not. Guo found specific variations in three genes that were associated with bad behavior, but only when the boys suffered other complex environmental stresses."

So it is true that some people, when confronted with difficulty, seem to be programmed, biologically, to be violent. Conversely, those who don't have these markers will respond to the same situation without violence. But that is not the full story, because many people who have these markers never express them—because they have never been placed into a situation where the genes have been triggered. Some are placed into those situations, but don't become violent due to support systems and training. There are also people who have these genes do behave violently, because they have been in violent and abusive circumstances.

The genetic markers for bad behavior are triggered by complex stressors and bad environments; that is to say, extreme violence can sometimes be a genetically amplified reaction to bad environments.

But what is a "bad environment?" That too, it turns out, has been studied. The strong predictors of violent expression are very specific kinds of poor parenting (regardless of socioeconomic status), with an emphasis on the following characteristics: "poor supervision; erratic, harsh discipline; parental disharmony; rejection of the child; and limited involvement in the child's activities." The second predictor is exposure to first-hand violence, and the third is exposure to media violence.

Researcher Bruce Perry states that "the most dangerous children are created by a malignant combination of experiences. Developmental neglect and traumatic stress during childhood create violent, remorseless children."

Kids with neglect and trauma have highly sensitized and poorly regulated brainstem systems, which results in a whole list of problems (anxiety, impulsivity, poor affect regulation, motor hyperactivity, low empathy, impaired problem-solving skills). Chaotic home environments and under-socialized development predispose these kids to all kinds of neuropsychiatric challenges and to violent behavior.

These kids have lost the neural circuitry needed to regulate their emotions. Richard Davidson says, "Normal individuals are able to voluntarily regulate their negative affect and can also profit from restraint-producing cues in their environment, such as facial and vocal signs of anger or fear, that also serve a regulatory role. Individuals predisposed to aggression and violence have developed abnormalities in the central circuitry responsible for these adaptive behavioral strategies."

For the component that is genetic, violent natures can be amplified by transgenerational selection. In violent societies, that is to say, there are more people with these genetic markers than nature would have on balance. It's a passive form of selective breeding.

Here is an example of how selective breeding works in the animal kingdom: In Russia, there is an ongoing experiment in which foxes have been bred for 20 generations. The breeders select the sweetest in the litter, and they also pick the most violently disposed, and then breed those animals separately. After 20 generations, the sweetest foxes were smart, kind house pets, and the violent foxes were so fierce that trainers could not approach their cages without the foxes trying to attack.

So there are a lot of damaged people out there who are now doing damage to others, often part of a multiple generation problem, perpetuating the cycle. What do we do?

Rewiring:
Can we change ourselves?

IT WOULD BE a terrible life sentence if our early experiences damaged us so much that we couldn't change. Luckily, science confirms that we are not stuck with the cards we are dealt. We have the capacity to change the make-up of our brains. In fact, our brains change whether we are consciously reprogramming them or not. Change is caused by the interplay between our genetic coding, our initial cultural programming, and what we encounter and choose every day.

What we feed into and how we "exercise" our brains is of equal value: our brains change in response to inputs and ideas. By giving the brain and body new experiences and new information, our circuitry is continually rewired. Just as repetitive motion builds a muscle's shape and capacity, flexible thinking and exposure to new places, people and things leads to a flexibly capable brain. The brain continues to evolve in response to circumstances throughout our lives—well into adulthood and beyond. The hippocampus of people well into their 60s increased in volume after they'd walked around a track three times per week for a year; in peers who did less aerobic exercises, the hippocampus actually got smaller.

This is called neuroplasticity: our experiences change both the brain's physical structure and its functional organization. Even small behavioral changes impact the brain: they don't have to be massive self-improvement or training efforts. Unlearning and reforming the brain is an ongoing process and occurs even with micro-shifts in activity.

Over time, these small changes can add up to major reconfigurations. Consider this study of city taxi drivers: Brain scans of new drivers,

drivers with 10 years' experience, drivers with 30 years experience showed an increase in the size and activity level in the hippocampus, the area of the brain that govern geospatial awareness. Substantial changes occur in the lowest neocortical processing areas, and these changes profoundly alter the pattern of neuronal activation in response to experience. Taxi drivers physically grow the appropriate part of their brains in correlation with the time they spend driving the streets.

Similarly, neuroimaging suggests that meditating for just 30 minutes a day for eight weeks can increase the density of gray matter in brain regions associated with memory, stress, and empathy.

Sensory perceptions, thoughts, and actions all drive chemical and electrical responses. Through this process, not only the brain, but the systems it directs—the nervous system, the endocrine system, in fact, the entire body—will reorganize and restructure themselves, strengthening and weakening where appropriate.

What this science suggests is that we are always faced with choices—and what we choose matters. We literally remake ourselves every day.

Building a more connected, less violent world *can be done*. We can accelerate our evolution as a species. To change and adapt, just as with software, we have to consciously debug ourselves. We need to release the preexisting programs that came bundled with our hardware. Then, we can put a new program in place and, over time, write a new code.

MEETING THE OTHER

One way to rewire: Changing our beliefs

MANY YEARS AGO my friend Ron Miller, who ran the theology department at Lake Forest College, came to speak with a small group of spiritual seekers about how to read the Bible in a more useful and accurate way.

He focused on two core themes. First, he discussed cultural context. Ron said that any Bible story had to be taken in its cultural context to really get at its true meaning. As an example, he used the often misinterpreted Proverb 13, the source of the aphorism "spare the rod, spoil the child." This proverb has been used to justify corporal punishment, but that's not what it meant in the time in which it was written. Rather, in its cultural context, this proverb refers to shepherds, who used their rods to keep their sheep from falling off cliffs and to keep the flock together—not to beat the animals. With this information taken into consideration, a better interpretation of the proverb would be that children need guidance and strong boundaries.

The second theme he invited us to consider was to distinguish between "pre-scientific" and "post-scientific" thinking in whatever story we read. The Bible, Miller said, was written within the context of a poetic, or pre-scientific, culture. It can't be read with a literal mind and be correctly understood. To illustrate this point, he used the example of trying to understand and make sense of a river from each of these two different mindsets.

If someone with a pre-scientific mindset were to approach a river, she might make aesthetic evaluations or ask practical questions: how beautiful it is, how does it fit into the overall environment, what is downstream, what it means, where do I cross it, where can I fish in it. She might taste it or even swim in it and get the feel of the water. These observations and engagements would create a personal, individualized direct experience of the river. A scientific mind, on the other hand, might categorize the type of river, assess its depth and velocity, calculate its power, assess the harvest potential. The river might be reduced it to quantitative abstract measures of utility: known in some ways, but not understood.

Here's another example. Early in my career I was working in mergers and acquisitions, and our client was buying steel mills and foundries. Found-ries make metal parts for cars and other machinery via a process called iron casting. In casting, hot iron is poured into a sand mold; then, as the iron hits the sand, it cools into the appropriate shape. In the process of learning about the industry, I talked to foundry workers who'd been on the job for 40 or more years. These men had such an intimate understanding of the nature of the sand. In order to evaluate whether the sand was the right blend and dampness for the iron to be poured, they would take a small ball of it, taste it, roll it around in their mouths, and then spit it out to see how it stuck to the wall. In short, they were approaching the casting process with a pre-scientific mindset—one driven not by quantifiable data, but by direct sensory experience. In the process of modernizing the factory with new equipment, those men were replaced with instruments that told the whether the sand was ready with only numbers; but the knowledge of the sand—how it tasted, how it felt—was in no way as complete.

In the pre-scientific age, individual components in a system were less important than the whole. Situations, places and even people were thought to influence each other through an interplay of forces. This holistic worldview created a tolerance for complexity and an allowance for the unexplainable and mysterious. It was organic and integrated. Recently, we've seen a reemergence of systems thinking, but it comes on the heels of many generations that had literally forgotten how to think that way.

I'm not saying that pre-scientific thinking was better—after all, it's also the mentality that produced witch-hunts and persecuted discoverers like Gali-leo. I'm inviting a consideration of what segregating complex interactions into compartmentalized simple interactions might have done to our worldview and culture.

The overall trajectory has led us from an inclusive, multi-sensory, direct experience of the world to abstraction, measurement and reductionism. Scientific thinking ushered in an unprecedented attempt to explore, explain, and master the natural world. All things were thought to be explainable.

As the dominant thought pattern moved from poetry to science, we began an attempt to catalog the known universe into neat little categories, called taxonomies, an idea that has since been applied to everything from books to insects: it teaches is to treat things as clearly defined, separate objects that can be arranged in a finite order. In the bigness of the universe, maybe humans increasingly sought to feel in control, and putting labels on things and breaking complex systems into their most finite parts sure is a great way to create an illusion of control or understanding. I have come to think that this way of thinking about objects and the natural world was a critical factor in how we have come to relate to each other as humans - as separated individual beings.

Ideas that separate: Taxonomic thinking

To workers I'm just another drone
To Ma Bell I'm just another phone
I'm just another statistic on a sheet
To teachers I'm just another child
To IRS I'm just another file
I feel like a number
I'm not a number, I'm not a number
Dammit I'm a man
I said I'm a man
— BOB SEGER, "FEEL LIKE a Number"

In the scientific, and then industrial mindset, an entire cohort of celebrated thinkers arose (Charles Darwin, Carl Linnaeus, Melvil Dewey, Frederick Taylor and Henry Ford, among others), all of whom tried to break systems and processes into their most speciated elements, and treat each element individually. This "taxonomic thinking" has its own genius, especially in the discernment of fine differences, and intensity of observed detail, but it also has a cost. It diminishes contextual juxtapositions and discoveries, reduces the perception of interdependence and oversimplifies reality. And of course the world doesn't actually work by these hard and fast rules categories; ecosystems, societies, even libraries are actually made up of complex intertwinings.

Consider how categorization works in a library. The Dewey Decimal System tells us exactly where to find a book based on broad information about topic and genre. But that's *all* it tells us. The system doesn't tell us anything about the style of the writing, the quality, the background of the author, the details in the illustrations. So if all we know about a book is its call number, we actually know very little about the book in its totality. The same is true for any individual element of a system: the taxonomic information simply tells us where to find things, not what they are. Just because we know where a thing fits doesn't mean we understand it.

This imposition of apparent order on unfathomable complexity is the cultural framework that Western thought has been steeped in for more than 100 years, and it's not a complete, nor even very helpful, story.

Seeing "individual things" and not intertwined environments sets up a whole false framework for thinking that individuals can act alone, or act without impact or dependency on surrounding systems.

Let's look back at Darwin for a moment. When Darwin organized animals into kingdom, phyla, genus, order and species in ever more finite detail, he wasn't simply categorizing. He was also trying to understand HOW nature organizes itself and WHY the living world is the way it is. Why did this bird's long beak evolve; why did this animal's pelt come to be; why those eye shapes; why that coloration? In looking at the *why* behind diversity in nature, he concluded that nature favored those that best fit their environment. For example, birds with longer beaks did better at finding insects in environments where bugs were hidden in crevices. He called this the "Survival of the Fittest." The "fittest" in Darwin's context meant, that which is most in harmony with its environment. Those who are best suited to their environment gain procreational advantage. Survival based on harmony is an organic process of adapting to the environment. Survival is not based upon who is the strongest as an individual!

Still, somewhere along the line, Darwin's theory was perverted. So-called Social Darwinists twisted survival of the fittest from harmony with the environment to a form of competition between members of an ecosystem for survival. This misinterpretation was offered as a "scientific" theory, and misapplied to justify the social abandonment of less advantaged human groups—"May the best man win!" is a natural expression of this social Darwinist attitude. In Social Darwinism, survival is based on competition between people or tribes; it relies on trying to get one up on the other person, and in seeking advantage over others.

The result of this worldview is predictable. If we think we are in competition with others for finite resources (e.g., food, shelter, mates), life is a constant struggle. Rather than existing as individuals engaged in a lifelong collaboration between affiliated beings, we are either better or worse than others based on how we are winning (or not) at any moment. But that was not Darwin's intention. Survival of the "fittest" in nature never meant survival of the "best." It never meant competition between individuals. By twisting the understanding of the scientific mechanism of Darwinism into the false model of Social Darwinism, we missed the opportunity to see that all of nature—including Homo sapiens—thrives when it is in harmony.

Categorizing and labeling isn't just about plants or books, it's been extended to people. Since the Industrial Revolution, we've been inching toward the increased widgetization of people—defining them by jobs and specialties, as if that's all they are. Maybe this has been going on for much longer. After all, there were classes and castes and guilds long before the first internal combustion engine rolled off the line. Yet, there is something in the anonymity of modern life and the increasing specialization of tasks that seems to further pigeonhole and simplify people. When Henry Ford pioneered efficient manufacturing, using assembly line techniques, wherein each person's work was studied, and through the use of motion assessments, the most efficient movements were prescribed—each person was to do it the best way, the right way, the only way- he was in part saying this is who you are, this is the part of the job you will do.

It seems to me that this thinking has seeped into our daily interactions, where we put each other into little boxes: *That woman is an accountant; I know what she's like. That man is from West Virginia; we won't have anything in common.*

When we label people they are diminished, pigeonholed, under-unappreciated. Labeling sets people up for a lifelong trajectory that may quickly outlive any initial usefulness.

In school, for example, kids who are labeled "gifted" often get tracked in the first year or two of their formal education. This identification builds on itself, with more challenging material and additional attention throughout their academic life. Recently, however, researchers have determined that if children are *not* placed on tracks early, they often swtich places - the so called average children catch up to their theoretically gifted peers. This practice of early labeling has major drawbacks—whether you're labeled as "gifted" or "regular", or even "special needs". If children are labeled as average or below average, they do not receive the same encouragement and challenge as those in gifted programs, and so they seldom perform to their highest abilities.

The initial label sets up a trajectory. It becomes, in effect, a self-fulfilling prophecy.

The damage to the labeled person is clear. But what about the person who does the labeling? What does the labeler lose? If we put others in a box, we run the risk of losing touch with reality and truth. Instead of seeing people as they are—complex, puzzling, surprising—we merely reinforce our stereotypes, becoming progressively more arrogant and misinformed. We miss out on opportunities for broader intersections with people: ways to connect on different levels and in unexpected domains. Put more simply, we miss out on friends. A new acquaintance probably won't want to hang out if she senses I'm not genuinely interested in her as a whole person.

Recently, I met a man who introduced himself saying "I'm a musician." It was only later in the dialogue that I found out he was also a venture investor of note. If we had started with the venture designation, I would probably have succumbed to my own "labeling," and never learned about his skills in voice and composition.

✳

If we rely solely on naked human observation, elephants seem fairly silent except for the occasional trumpeting. But that perception of stillness is not true. Elephants emit pervasive low frequency rumbles—for the human ear to hear the sound at all, it must be sped up thirty fold. They are in constant communication with other herds, their sound traveling hundreds of miles, signaling food supply, danger, territorial boundaries, mating opportunities. So it is with whale song, bird calls, cricket chirps. Language patterns like these are challenging for us to observe, but if we believe that what we see or hear is all there is, we are totally wrong. Our very biology limits our perception, so we can't rely solely on our senses to understand what's real; that's why we use microscopes and telescopes to see beyond our capacity and amplifiers and frequency modulators to hear beyond our ears. There is much more happening at any given time than we can take in and understand. Like faraway herds, everything in the perceivable world is much more interconnected than we observe. Whether we are aware of it or not, we are interdependent, interwoven and always playing on the seen and unseen energies of others.

✳

Can we even know what's really happening?

THE WESTERN WORLDVIEW, for the most part, teaches that we are independent, individual beings. In our system, our worth comes primarily from what we produce. We are always being graded by others, and our worth and security are wrapped up in how well we conform to what they expect

While I was raised with this perspective, as I grew up, moving from inherited experiences to experiences that I chose for myself, I realized that these separatist teachings felt fundamentally untrue. My direct experience was one of increasing interdependence, interconnection and complexity. Each person was infinitely more layered than I had ever imagined.

I decided to question how I had lost touch with myself and others. Beyond that, I wanted to know to how we, as a culture, had lost touch with our interdependence in the first place. I wanted to know if we could collectively "hack" our own evolution, and the evolution of the collective? Could we speed up our enlightenment and reduce some suffering along the way? What if everything we had taken in unconsciously was up for discussion? If we give ourselves permission to question, alone and with others, we might design any manner of new ways to live.

If we go through our lives unconsciously, the neurons and atoms that make us up will continue to play out their repeating code. But if we become conscious, we can use every bit of information we have about how we work—historical, sociological or scientific—to help us rewire ourselves, as well as the culture we live in.

I've found that approaching this questioning of what's broken in our culture with a heart of compassion toward the institutions under inquiry, rather than a mindset of attack and critique, helps a lot.

I see it this way: all systems are exquisite adaptations. They are contextual and place bound; they arose naturally to meet the very real needs of the time in which they were created. But as time and circumstance changed, many institutions overstayed their welcome, couldn't adapt or change, and ossified.

When there's a problem with the dominant culture, and we have the enthusiasm for reconnection and redesign, and we also join that enthusiasm with loving rather than destructive intent, we are using the force of our intention to create systemic change. In doing so, we can honor and celebrate what we've learned so far, and give it an honorable retirement. It is unlikely that the whole society be willing to look together and release what isn't working— but that some will want to hold on tight, as if they can't handle the coming change. That is where courage comes in.

This process of questioning and reinventing may be difficult, but the result is more than worth the effort.

Simply by being members of a culture (and this is true of any culture, though here I only consider Western traditions), we inherit a slew of beliefs and ideologies. Some of these may be useful; others, not so much. I want to avoid simply internalizing ideas handed down to me by previous generations. Instead, I want to interrogate inherited ideas, find out if they work for me, for *us*, and if they don't, I want to see what else is out there.

There are as many ways of conducting this inquiry as there are people. The methods I chose were research and exploration. I started reading and asking questions of neuroscientists, of behavioral psychologists, of historians. What does science, old or new, tell us about beliefs I've taken for granted? What new advances are we making on how the human organism functions? What do we know about tribalism, violence, love? Then I compared these findings to my own real-world encounters with humans. As I merged these two ways of seeking and knowing, a beautiful weaving begin to occur in my understanding: The heart and mind in equal balance, I realized, create an integration richer than either would be alone.

Here are two examples of science providing new bits of information can wake up and create a change of heart, a change in belief.

First, a story about mercury dental fillings in children. In the past decades, many parents said *adamantly* that their kids were increasingly having learning disabilities since their children received mercury fillings. The American Dental Association conducted a study, but found no correlation between mercury and such disabilities. The parents accused the ADA of being in denial and motivated by greed. The ADA responded that the parents were, essentially, imagining things, that there was no evidence to support their fears. The human story was all about judgment and blame.

Then, a new bit of data surfaced. It was shown that that certain children have a genetic marker for mercury sensitivity. When the data about learning challenges and mercury exposure were rerun, with the genetic marker information as a new variable, there was indeed a direct relationship between mercury and learning delays. If a child had such genetic markers, he or she predictably had developmental delays of up to five years, depending on the number of markers present and the number of mercury encountered. If the child didn't have the markers, there was no correlation at all. The scientists hung their heads; the data validated the parents' experience. The parents could say: the study wasn't conducted with ill intent. This was an opening here for both sides to say, "I was right, and I was also wrong—at the same time."

A second example of new science changing social belief comes from studies of the minds of criminals. Our justice system is based on free will. We call people who are violent "animals," and we think they are making a choice. This leads to a tremendous amount of judgment and shaming. But recent findings in science show that children who are serially traumatized (especially before the age of seven) often lose function in the part of their brains that can put a cushion between stimulus and response; that part of the brain goes dark. Their free will is literally limited. More than 80% of people in prison *were* severely traumatized as children before the age of seven. How does this new finding inform our sense of connection to these perpetrators, and our sense of what the right response from the culture is? Now that I know this I lean to restorative justice, rather than punitive justice. I more often lead with empathy.

Information like this can help us craft better responses to loneliness, argument, disconnection and violence. In the dental example, who did you side with before the genetic data was added to the picture? In the criminal example, did knowing the brain was damaged bring any reframing of the problem in your mind?

We now know that our interactions with others are governed by a wide array of things we are given (genetics, culture, family stories, experiences), and the things we seek out (learning, practices, alternate viewpoints, people, places and things). We have accepted so much of what is optional as fixed. When we start to do this work on ourselves, and reframe how we see the other, it cascades into all the realms of our life: our romantic relationships, our parenting, our communities, how we work together and how we govern.

In my experience, those who are seeking more connection and continuous reinvention are happier. They are open. They know that it is the separation that is the lie; the union is the true thing. These are people who are at ease with each other, even in conflict. They are egalitarian and able to equally commune with all. They are the ones for whom there is always a couch to sleep on, a table to sit at, a band to jam with.

I wanted to know this in my bones, not only conceptually. I wanted to investigate how will we might move fully into our own lives, evolve and grow, rethink our assumptions, float above our judgments, and redesign things that aren't working. What could I learn about disconnection and connection? About choosing to be perpetrators or healers? Who was already successful in creating a more loving and interwoven world?

Talking to strangers

I BECAME ACUTELY aware of my own prejudices one summer while traveling. We were visiting the strikingly desolate and beautiful White Sands National Monument in Alamogordo, NM. There we spoke with a rancher running a roadside fruit stand, a blue-eyed sheep farmer offering apple juice and pecan butter. None of my Spidey-senses were up; he looked just like me. But you know what we got with that pecan butter? A big helping of virulent, hateful, racist, fundamentalist worldviews that emerged over the course of the conversation.

Later that day, I was getting a coffee, and the register printed out a free video rental bonus coupon, so I turned to give it to the person behind me who might be local and able to use it. As I turned, I found myself looking at the bare chest of a tall, wild-haired, missing-toothed guy in a leather biker vest. Startled by his appearance, I took a deep breath, made eye contact, and started a conversation. He was from Nova Scotia, a Scotsman by heritage. He told me that he coordinates the local AA meetings, and is a Big Brother. I learned that his philosophy is to love one another; we are all the same beneath our skin. Little did het know, but he started me on an ongoing project that I call "Talking to Strangers."

The project involved a conscious attempt to find the person in any room who scared me the most, or that I had the most prejudices about, and begin a conversation with them. It's too easy to just say "the world is scary" and live with the goal of protecting myself from the unknown, from any potential danger. Instead I kept asking, "What is really happening here? Who is this person, really?"

Kayley

A S TALKING TO strangers unfolded, I met so many people who challenged my assumptions. On one roundtrip drive from the Bay Area to Tacoma, a good 700 miles in each direction, I picked up riders (a.k.a. hitchhikers, or travelers) going north and south. It was a first. Maybe it was awareness of the hard times and struggles of people everywhere I look that made me more open. Maybe it was feeling the shame of a nearly empty car, emitting CO_2 on behalf of one lonely driver.

There seemed to be a lot of travelers on the road at that time, more than during other driving trips I had done. Every intersection I stopped at had someone flying a sign with the direction they were headed, announcing what they needed or had to offer. Some were students or backpackers on their *wanderjahr*; some were lifestyle travelers, having chosen to live itinerantly; some just seemed down on their luck. I had to remind myself that no matter how these travelers appeared, I couldn't actually know why they were out there unless I asked them. Each one had unique reasons, unique struggles, unique desires that had led them to be waiting by the highway shoulder with a square of ragged cardboard.

There are biases and -isms in America for any group of people you can imagine, but there are few groups so simultaneously judged and ignored as the poor, the mobile, the homeless. Most of the homeless are crazy, they want something from you, they should get a job—the pre-judgments go on and on.

On my way north, I picked up a young couple in their mid-20s and their dog. The man was in camouflage, and the woman wore jeans with jingle bells around her ankles. The guy fell asleep immediately. The girl, Kayley, and I talked the rest of the time. She was tan and bright-eyed and dirty from sleeping outside, but very articulate. She'd been on the road for nine months, cutting across from Michigan, making a big circle up to the Rainbow Gathering in the mountains near Washington State, working the cleanup and restoration crew. They were on the way to Montana on this leg of their journey. Before she started wandering she had worked two jobs, in an Outback Steak House and in an office. She had a rented condo, and owned a car. The car broke down, one of the jobs ended, her boyfriend was a deadbeat and didn't pay his share—the numbers weren't adding up. So she broke her lease and decided to hit the road, see America. "I'm better fed, safer, have made better friends, and feel happier living like this than I did working two jobs in Detroit."

Some people are on the road by choice.

Spending time with Kayley gave me an appetite to do that again—to reach out to others who might not be in a position to go to Hertz or Amtrak or Southwest or even Craigslist. So on the way back, driving south on Interstate 5 near the Oregon border, I picked up Jack and Annie.

Jack

JACK WAS A 54-year-old man, and his dog was named Annie. Jack wore a leather hat and hiking sandals and carried one small pack, a jug of water, and a donut cushion to sit on. He had no tent. He'd been on a painting gig up in Seattle, fallen off the ladder, and broken his tailbone. He was tired. He'd been standing at this onramp for three days waiting for a ride south, where he thought he could find work and get support from some people he knew.

While we drove, he talked. Jack was from a teeny town twenty miles from Enterprise, Alabama. The son of farm hands, he'd been working since he was ten. "I'm a worker," he told me. "I want to work, but there's no work anywhere around. Everybody's hanging on to their money nowadays." He lived in the migrant camps and picked cotton. He hadn't gone past the first grade, but he could read, he told me, "kind of slowly." His mother had left when he was two, and his dad believed street smarts mattered more than book learning. He wondered who he would have been if he'd had an education. "No one in my family has two nickels to rub together." Still, in some assertion that he was still a participating citizen, he was careful to tell me that he has a driver's license, State Farm insurance on his truck that broke down, and a cell phone (but no charger). Until recently he'd been the driver, not the rider.

His pride was wounded. He was profoundly depressed at being broke, injured and without work. "If it weren't for my dog," he told me, "who knows?" He had named her Lil' Orphan Annie, and raised her from a pup. Before that, he had a dog named Paisano, who had a hole in his left ear from when his prior owner tried to kill him and the bullet missed. He'd had that dog for fifteen years, "a real good dog."

If he sees something, Jack told me, he can put it on paper or sculpt it. He likes working in pastels and doing portraits. He had no art supplies, but hoped to pick some up when he got to where he was going. Then he could do street corner portraits; that usually led somewhere. "I've done signs and murals all over. Christmas is a good time, 'cause I paint Christmas windows at shops."

Jack noticed everything as we drove. Birds on the reservoir balancing on the tip of a submerged tree limb. Rock cairns 100 feet away. Marijuana growing under blue tarps. He narrated the highway work going on around us, the techniques being used to straighten the road through the mountains.

He hoped to find enough work in Northern California to save up $1,500 for a camper he'd seen for sale last spring, when he was sealing the exterior walls of a wooden cabin. "Maybe I'll clean bud," he said. "People are coming from all over the country to do that job right about now. You can make $200 for cleaning a pound—and if you're fast, you can clean a pound a day." He hoped the camper was still for sale. "It's right on the highway, at my friend Larry's. That's where you can drop me off."

We got to Larry's place. It was a natural cedar house with a green roof. "You should meet him," John said. "Come on." There were gnomes and plumbing parts and assorted rock piles in the front yard. Larry was in a wheelchair; he had been shot while serving in Vietnam. He was leathered and had open, awake eyes.

Jack and Larry started to talk, catching up in general. Then Jack asked about the camper.

"Yes, it's still for sale. But there's a family of six living in there now, a husband and wife and their four babies. You can't take the camper until they find somewhere to go. They were in Minnesota 'cause he found work there, and that didn't pan out, and they came back with nowhere to live and no money. Hard times. So they're staying here."

I looked up at the rise next to the house where there were three or four campers and conversion vans. A young woman was watching two toddlers play with a faded Tyco slide set.

Larry's door opened and closed as people come in and out. He started in on America, how hard times are. "We should be bringing all troops home from overseas engagements, putting them to work on a new WPA, roads and infrastructure and schools and closing the borders and getting our own house in order. Everyone needs work, and there's no work. And now that the terrorists in Washington are using the budget and the debt ceiling as a threat to the people, there won't be any until after the 2012 elections. It may have been the Congress, but I heard coming from Obama's mouth that they may cut off social security checks and veterans benefits, and even if that was an empty threat, people got scared. Any cash they might have spent got stuck to the insides of their wallets. Not even paying people to do odd jobs." He used the word "nigger". He went on, saying, "Michelle Bachmann is interesting. Maybe I'll vote for her; she raised 28 kids."

Jack was uncomfortable, seeming to sense a class clash coming. Though I was a guest in this house for the moment, all I wanted to say was, *Did you really just say "nigger?" Do you not realize this is the 21st century?*

I was shaken by the time we left. I understood what Mark Twain had meant when he wrote, "Travel is fatal to prejudice, bigotry, and narrow-mindedness, and many of our people need it sorely on these accounts. Broad, wholesome, charitable views cannot be acquired by vegetating in one little corner of the earth all one's lifetime."

I decided to take Jack a little farther, to Fortuna, just south of Eureka. There we would part ways, and I would continue home. He wanted to show me a mural he'd done, one he told me about earlier. It was a block off the highway in Eureka, which he called Eurtweaka, because of all the kids tweaked out on meth, the lost children of rural America, cranked and crazy. He pointed out the flophouses and talked about how the police in Arcata and Eureka run you off if they sense you are a vagrant. The sure sign is having any kind of backpack.

The mural was immense; coconut palms and surf and an island landscape ran the full length of a building. In front, on an empty gravel lot, the landscaper had constructed a fake island, complete with rises and plants and giant Buddha sculptures and ramshackle buildings and tiki torches. There was live music and some cackling coming from inside.

Jack hollered at the wooden gates, "Hey, is Mitch here?"

"Who wants to know?" A greasy little hunched-over middle-aged white guy in a sarong appeared, smiling broadly and showing blackened and missing teeth. Even with the smile, he looked threatening. But when John informed him that he was the one who'd painted the mural, the man's tone changed immediately. "Let me show you around. My name is Tim." There were giant exotic plants, little bridges, lanterns mixed in with cracked couches and broken aluminum lawn furniture. Despite the change in tone, all of my alarm bells on safety were going off: the barbed wire fences, the alarm system, the agitation in the man's eyes, I was encountering a new side of Talking to Strangers: it can be put you in legitmately alarming situations. Bravery and naivete are not the same thing.

Some people are on the road via circumstance.

I could have taken the same old road that day, and floated past all the parts of the world and the people that I would otherwise never have seen, remaining oblivious, wondering, or judging. It wasn't all positive, this exploration; most of the explorations weren't. They were showing me, up close and personal, the alternate realities of my fellow citizens. My penniless hitch-hiker had turned out to be a gifted itinerant artist. And that sunny landscape he'd crafted masked a dark underside of addiction and closed-mindedness inside the building it was painted on. *Keep looking*, I thought. *Pay exquisite attention. You never know what's around the corner, or inside the next doorway.*

Chuck

PEOPLE'S STORIES OF how far they'd come from their origins were the most humbling of all. I met Chuck in the summer of 2014, when we rented a RV from him for a Nevada road trip. He was in his late sixties, ruddy and white bearded, a former music-store owner. He rented us an old ramshackle RV, which fell apart while we were out in the desert: the bed collapsed, the AC didn't work, the water smelled, and the engine died; it got a "do not resuscitate" order. We left it in out in the big wide dusty wilderness for him to retrieve, and took a car back to his house in Sun Valley to pick up our belongings.

When we finally got to Chuck's cement holding yard with the cyclone fencing, my traveling companion had to take a conference call, pacing around the lot for a long hour. So I sat on the wooden stoop just observing. Chuck had four or five little dogs—poodles and spaniels and a terrier. I held the back of my hand out, as I had been taught to do with strange dogs, and waited for them to come over. Eventually, they did. Once they felt safe they were friendly and rambunctious, running around my feet in circles.

I asked Chuck, "How'd you get them?"

"The little one there I took from a man, because she was six pounds under the weight she is now," he told me. "Her fur was matted and had barbed wire in it. It was so bad that I took the dog from the owners' arms and called animal control. I said, 'Listen, you got to come over. I got to show you something,' and they came. Animal control said, 'Is that even a dog?' I said, 'yes.' I told them I am not giving him back to the owner, and I am not giving him to you. I am going to take care of him. But I want you to see the condition in which I received this puppy.' "

I asked how he came to be so vigorous in his defense of this dog. He paused, as if deciding how much to tell.

He said, "Well, I grew up in West Virginia. The people were poor and uneducated. My father, like a lot of others, was a drunkard. One night, when I was nine, he walked in the door staggering. He looked at my dog and said, 'I don't like the looks of that dog. You take that dog up on the top of the hill, and shoot it.'

"Now, in that time and place, you didn't say 'no' to your father. So I did it. I walked into the woods and I shot that dog. But at that moment, a switch flipped in me. I vowed that day that I would never take another life. Since I moved to Nevada, I have saved over a hundred dogs in Sun Valley. None of that," he said, "can wash away shooting the dog that I shot when I was nine. But I never laid a hand on anything or anyone after that."

How do some people become disconnected to the point of harming one another, while others become healers? Is it grace? Are some people born one way, or do we develop the skills to be a certain way? Is enacting a life of compassion and connection an acquired skill, or one that's bestowed upon us? Can we find a way to shift our own evolution away from destructive tendencies, and to a new place of creativity, generosity and connection?

"Othering"

WHEN I ASK people about their lives I step out of myself and my stories, experiences and beliefs and try another perspective on for size. In asking and not assuming, I'm trying to see, respect, and love others actively—to see all people as equally valuable and unique expressions of the creative force of the universe, not better or worse basd on some label.

For many of us, our identity is made up of all kinds of labels: race, ethnicity, religion, class, education, marital, employment or parental status. These can be great fun as affinity groups, and offer a sense of belonging and understanding. But when identification with a group turns into *this is who I am*, it becomes a tool for separating from others.

If we classify or filter people into groups, we can't help but compare: The label allows me to say *you are not like me*. But even this in and of itself isn't a problem. The problem comes when one's own "identifiers" are preferred, or deemed to be better. Maybe even the best.

It's in this critical moment of assigning value to the label that "othering" becomes dangerous and distancing. In othering, we turn people into objects, into catalog units, less than my friends and me, and sometimes even less than human. If we live in segregated communities, or hang out with people mostly like ourselves, the problem is intensified. In many cases, it's in the attempt to define ourselves that we distance from the other.

Othering is at the root of why we are so fragmented. It's the reason we are able to say, "You are not like me. You don't share my values. You are less than I am. Therefore, I can treat you poorly. I can hurt you, and it's justified." This is the essence of the hate crime, the gang crime, misogyny, of internet trolls and bullies.

How do we get around this? After all, we've been othering more or less since the day we started pre-school. In my extended family, when adults saw a black person, they would whisper the Hungarian word for "black". It was uncultured to say it in English, but they still were thinking it. And who among us didn't go to an educational institution where the rules of the clique dominated?

If our own identity and worth comes exclusively from any label (I'm an American, I'm a man, I'm a soldier, I'm fighting the holy war, I'm from the South Side), then any opposing viewpoint, criticism or contradiction is a potential threat. The more we identify with our chosen or given labels, the more others' choices might become an assault or impingement on our own worth.

Our identity must expand, we must start to view ourselves as independent of all of these labels, and intrinsically valuable—as are all others. Our prejudices toward each other impeded our evolution to a more just and joyful society for all. They are a threat to the collective connection.

When I started this practice of talking to strangers, I wanted to know their histories, of course: what they thought, why they thought it. I also wanted to know about myself: where was my life being limited by my fear: Where was I inviting disconnection because of my own assumptions? Where do I still hold prejudice? Was I willing to take a risk to find out if they were right? Or was I going to be too afraid to take that risk, and stay in my box? Anytime I can make a sentence like "men are like this" or "Chinese people are like this," I know I'm dealing with something deep-seated in my encoded beliefs. How do I knock those out so that I can actually see what is real in the individual that I'm encountering? How do we really meet, see and learn people's truths? How do I show up with questions, rather than with fear or blame? Talking to strangers, really seeing them, has become the practice of a lifetime.

As I listened and watched as people told me about their journeys—how they think and what they've seen. Just in the way they spoke, I could detect an exposition of the underlying belief structures that were driving them. I had to be aware of phrases they used and the things they said, because their ways of speaking captured certain qualities of their lives. And capturing that dialogue meant I had captured that space in time, captured at least a snapshot of who these people were.

In the end, the hunger for knowing and growing was stronger than the need to keep myself comfortable or even safe?

RETHINKING COMMUNITY

It takes a community to raise a consciousness; it takes community to raise a relationship; it takes community to raise a family. I could go on: to heal the planet, to care for the aged or infirm, to raise a barn or make a choir. The connections that come without transaction, that arise through reclaiming tribe, are the juiciest bits of being human.
— KELLY BRYSON

A small stage in Monterey

W ITH NO FLAIR, little finesse, no dressing for success, nothing external to suggest ambition in the corporate sense, Aubrey de Grey digs deeper and deeper into his question.

"What if aging is not a condition, but a disease?" he asks from the stage. "Why should the body die, anyway?" de Grey fits his name: just over forty, he is a serious, stately man with a long, mountain-man beard. He has pioneered an entirely new framing of longevity and has opened up a new field of study. He is also one of the men behind the Methuselah Mouse Prize, which rewards discoveries in life extension research.

As I listen to de Grey—with several hundred other audience members— what impresses me even more than his search for "un-death" is his personal commitment to the question. He postulates with authenticity, and an inner strength of conviction. Listening to him, I feel energy course through my body; it is as if I am waking from a long slumber.

In February 2004, a friend invited me to attend the Technology, Entertainment and Design Conference in Monterey. Widely known as TED, it is an annual gathering of thinkers across multiple disciplines from around the world. When I attended, TED had not yet become the global movement it is today, with groundbreaking talks streaming on the web and local organizers hosting spinoff events all over the world.

At that time I was doing some interesting work in cloud computing, which fit the "T" part of the equation. But otherwise, beyond being there to meet people, I wasn't sure how or why I fit the scene.

The same day I heard de Grey speak, I watched Al Gore discuss horrifying data on climate change. I listened to Majora Carter, a young activist from the Bronx, talk about her work with *Greening the Ghetto*—turning a poisonous dump into a park. Larry Brilliant, a public health pioneer, talked about using Google and other search engines to predict outbreaks of pandemic diseases.

At some point Sheila Patek, a marine biologist, stood on stage, gesticulating broadly, with an equally broad grin. She explained her discovery: the miracle of nature that is the hammer shrimp, which boasts the highest power to size mechanism in nature. I watched her motion-capture video, slowed to frame by frame, dissecting the motions and structures that generated this power. Shrimp aside, I was moved by Sheila's sheer curiosity, her joy in the dedicated pursuit of an investigation with no promised rewards. The guilelessness and purity of her sharing. What made her follow this spring-loaded creature? What prompted her to look?

As each person rose to speak, I was increasingly moved to grateful and reflective silence at their clarity of intent. Where and how had each found their purpose? How did they disconnect from the frame of dominant values to pursue that purpose? Where did these people get the idea that divergent thinking is not only a legitimate path, but maybe the only path?

I hadn't wanted anything in a long time—but sitting in that audience, it seemed to me that these people, these thinkers and creators, were models for the way I wanted to live my own life: in inquiry and investigation, instead of suffocated in micro tasks and consumer distractions. I wanted this way of being. The TED presenters were shining a bright light onto the importance of questioning the status quo, and of being unceasingly curious about *the way things really work* and *the way things could be.*

Burning away the "default world"

DRIVE OUT PAST Nevada's Pyramid Lake, through the Paiute Reservation, and far, far from the casinos. Eventually you will arrive at a prehistoric lakebed in the middle of the desert, governed by the Bureau of Land Management. Add tens of thousands of people, all adhering to bold principles of experimental community, and, like me, you may be amazed at what blooms.

In 2004, a few months after I attended TED, my friend Bryan from California invited me his camp at Burning Man. The theme that year was "The Vault of Heaven." I signed up. A month before we were to leave for Black Rock Desert, he told me that he'd have to return to India unexpectedly. "Christine, you're on your own. I'm sorry. But this camp is made up of great people; you will really like them. Just be open."

I knew nothing about the area or the Burning Man culture or its people. I knew not a single soul, other than Maria, who was taking the same route from Chicago as I was, also a first timer. I had taken a "responsible role" in organizing our camp prior to the festival, coordinating meals for 80 people. But I did very poor research. I thought it would be a big party in the desert. When I heard "desert," I thought sand dunes. So I packed a tent and a sleeping bag, flew into Reno, got water and a bike, and headed out to Black Rock City (BRC), the heart of the Black Rock Desert. Instead of a soft, sandy surface, it was hard-packed alkaline, rock solid. I was unequipped—without goggles or a mask—for the frequent wind and dust storms. The intensity of these storms created a dramatic, post-apocalyptic landscape.

After arriving, there's no use of personal cars until departure. You can walk, run, dance, ride a bike, or climb onto a 'mutant vehicle.' These vehicles, which needed to be registered ahead of time, were art projects in themselves. Some were decorated as miniature cupcakes and only fit one person. There was a mammoth Noah's Ark mounted on a truck bed; to ride it, you had to be dressed as an animal. In other years, there was a giant disco duck on a truck chassis, a five-masted copper pirate ship; a city bus wrapped in silks and lit from within. At night, the bus looked like a giant glow-worm crawling across the desert.

Around my camp were giant baskets of lingerie and evening gowns and crazy costumes that people had collected over the years. The goal was to simply find something that expresses you. I was a woman coming out of wearing a business suit everyday. I ended up wearing a lacy, extravagant white dress with leafy headbands and other accessories: the feminine essence, flowing and at ease. In fact people were dressed in every manner, from Mad Max to Steam Punk. Men dressed in sheer lingerie, and girls wore loin-cloths during the day and pink fur with neon trim at night. Others dressed in nothing but silver body paint—or just nothing at all.

If the TED culture was about planning ahead, about meeting people, at Burning Man any notion of strategy was completely absent. The only strategy on entering this community was to march towards freedom, co-creation, expression. These men and women were yearning for a different culture, where people interacted under an entirely new context. There is nothing to get from anyone else; there is only giving to other people. At the time I first went to these two events, there wasn't a big convergence of the TED and Burning Man people—today there are. Although there is a big difference in the cultural modeling, the people both attract are both pulled by alternative ways of living.

At Burning Man, there's no access to any of the protections of social status that exist in day-to-day civilization. For me that meant no business cards, no suit, no handbag, no car, no title. At Burning Man, you are just you and your mostly naked self, and your currency is the way you treat the strangers around you. The more authentic you are, the richer your experience. Whatever feels like the most genuine way to interact, you do that.

Following that ethos, the whole purpose was to embrace the freedom and figure out what I could give to the community. That first day, it dawned on me that nobody was telling me what to do, where to go, when to wake up, what to eat. I'd had four kids at home for the past nineteen years, so I had to ask myself: What do I actually want to express? What do I actually feel? What is my gift? I spent the next few days investigating. I was in a vacuum, surrounded by 35,000 other men, women and children in the middle of the desert; this was where I experienced freedom.

I decided that I wanted to get up early, because I don't like to rave all night and I honor the sunrise. My gift to the camp would be in giving yoga classes on demand, whenever someone felt the need. I would go out into an open spot on the playa and put up a sign that said, "personalized yoga right now," and I would move people through a 15-minute practice and send them on their way.

In our camp alone, there were eighty people. They were the most open people I had ever met. I was stunned by the amount of affection and touching and play initiated without the usual tentative small talk. The camp was centered around open friendship, open love, just goofing off, and playing for a week for no reason.

Our camp was one of the original founding groups of Burning Man. They had participated since 1994, and were the founders and organizers of the famed "Critical Tits Ride," in which 10,000 women rode topless from one point of the playa to the other as a proclamation of female pride and gender celebration in every form.

After the first couple of days, it was clear that one of the things newcomers to the festival experience is the inability to say 'no' to events or ideas. Everything is done in the name of freedom and expression, so personal boundaries are weakened. While everything is experimental, and people are encouraged to tune into what feels right for them, that mindset can also be taken advantage of—even here there are predators.

One woman in our camp took it upon herself to make sure everyone had everything they needed—that they were provisioned, had costumes, and had somewhere they could go with questions. She was in her 40s, with the voice of a child and very open eyes, and open heart, and lots of wrinkles. She looked like she had lived hard and aged intensely. She took me under her wing.

In their daily lives, Burners aren't oddballs: they are surgeons, programmers, students, teachers, contractors. But they manage to maintain their devotion to making and creating the magnificent art projects and installations to share at the festival. Some do it as a side gig all year long. Peoples' imaginations are expansive, and their creations blew my mind: gigantic structures growing out of the desert floor or suspended in the air. Each project has its own purpose, but at the center of it all is the recognition that we humans have a natural instinct to create and express ourselves.

Over the years the art of Burning Man has been stunning. One year there was an installation called *Big Rig Jig*: two oil tankers suspended vertically, like two scorpions stinging one another from the tail. There were beautiful 20-story statues of dancing women, made out of wire mesh. One guy built a mobile projection lab in an old submarine. He would pull up near a camp, turn on his immense sound system, and project images onto whatever surface was available. Another man carved a section out of his welding business during the year to make a giant, illuminated metal heart. In 2014, there was a stunning wooden sculpture of a man and woman embracing. They emerged from the desert floor from the chest up, and reached several stories high. You could climb inside of it—and feel the couples conjoined, shared heart.

Every year there is a Temple. One year it was a massive, intricate structure resembling a post-apocalyptic Taj Mahal; its mimicry of lacey stonework was made of die-cut wooden jigsaw puzzle remnants.

The temple and the other art installations were built upon daily, until the final day. Some get repurposed after the event and find permanent homes, but almost all of the art is burned at the end of the week. There is an impermanence to the thing, pushing us to confront questions about our creative and destructive impulses. Why do we build? Why do we create beauty and deliberately destroy it? At Burning Man, attendees live in a transient environment, and we create because it is in our nature—despite the knowledge that it will all be burned in the end.

In the midst of our group camp was a common space for conversation and chilling out. An artist named Ping had built a three-tiered teepee-like structure in the space. It was wide at the base, and as you moved upward you entered a Mylar shade structure. Clear, transparent disks were suspended from above. There were 13 disks in total, facing downward, and etched into each disk was the symbol of one of the world religions. One disk, the last, was blank.

As the sun rose and set throughout the day along its cycle, its rays passed over each image so that each religious symbol projected, in turn, onto the Mylar. Over the course of each full day, each one of the religions dominated. By the time it got to the thirteenth symbol, there was emptiness: space for a religion yet to be envisioned.

In the center of this teepee structure was a suspended chair, attached to a pulley and lever system. The idea was to get in the chair and have someone hoist you all the way to the top, above the discs, above their religious images, until you could get a full view from above of all thirteen rings. The experiment sought to suggest that, to get a full picture, you must rise above your dogma. Ping called it *the dogmatron*.

At times during that first week, I felt bewildered and midwestern. I started to realize that my bewilderment was almost always related to my discomfort in my own skin. I was in my 30s and active, but I had so much body shame that the idea of being naked, flaws and all, was impossible for me. I was trying to stay cool the first couple of days, but also covered, and I was as anxious as I could be.

On my third day, one of the men from our camp, James, came up to me and asked, "What's up, Christine? You seem uneasy—trying to stay all covered up. Want to talk about it?"

So we sat on cushions in the shade, and he asked me questions. I told him how uncomfortable I was with my body. He suggested an exercise for us to try—non-sexual, he assured me—and I agreed.

Along the very far edge of the event is a fence that runs the full perimeter of Burning Man. It keeps trash and debris from blowing out into the desert. Here we were basically alone, away from passersby. James led me in a guided meditation. I took off every stitch of clothing, and stood in the bright sunlight with my eyes closed. First we focused on feeling the sun. Then on moving around and the sensations that produced. Then we looked: What did I see? How would I describe this part of me or that part of me? What was reality, what was story, what was judgment?

I said, "My toes are even and short. The second toe is shorter than the first. And because people with long second toes are noble stock, my feet show that I am of low status."

He said, "I see feet that are finely shaped, perfectly balanced and that hold your body up. I appreciate their arches, and that you can spread your toes."

I said, "My legs are not long enough, and they are too thick."

He said, "I see an athlete, with power and strength. A skater or a gymnast."

I said, "I have stretch marks."

He said, "Yes, I see them. They exist. So what? What does that mean to you?"

The experience wasn't about beauty in the abstract, aesthetic sense. It was about appreciation and awe for the wholeness of the body, even its perceived flaws. James wanted to show me what it felt like to be free in my own body, and he did.

I felt completely grateful and in love with my body, having the revelation, "Oh my god, look at the things that my body does!" For the first time in my adult life I stood as naked as a wild thing, naked in the open air, naked in the sunshine.

Another model

THE COMPETITIVE MODEL of human nature was not much in evidence at Burning Man. I was surrounded by people who were convinced that there is another way to live. Even though it's a contained and temporary environment, this gave me hope that we could shift our culture. We can set new principles and live by them. This possibility is not utopian science fiction.

If I look at how my experiences during my time at Burning Man, I can see that a chain of opportunities presented itself to me. I can see how one random conversation led to a meeting, which led to an invitation, which led to a life-changing moment.

It reminded me that all around us are people who say, "Hey, look over here! Look at what I've discovered!" Or they tell us about a thought they're having, and if we listen to them, they take us on amazing journeys. We get to go through the looking glass with them. We can also *be* that person for others. It matters, then, if we are open to hearing these people call us over to what they are seeing or thinking.

But, if we're stuck on our own agenda, those opportunities will feel diversionary for us. We miss out. Can we each be a 'yes' for those kinds of invitations?

BURNING MAN'S TEN PRINCIPLES

Burning Man is a living experiment in a new form of community, and what I experienced wasn't random, but rather a byproduct of intentional community design.
(© Burning Man Organization)

» **Radical Inclusion**: Anyone may be a part of Burning Man. We welcome and respect the stranger. No prerequisites exist for participation in our community.

» **Gifting**: Burning Man is devoted to acts of gift giving. The value of a gift is unconditional. Gifting does not contemplate a return or an exchange for something of equal value.

» **Decommodification**: In order to preserve the spirit of gifting, our community seeks to create social environments that are unmediated by commercial sponsorships, transactions, or advertising. We stand ready to protect our culture from such exploitation. We resist the substitution of consumption for participatory experience.

» **Radical Self-reliance**: Burning Man encourages the individual to discover, exercise and rely on his or her inner resources.

» **Radical Self-expression**: Radical self-expression arises from the unique gifts of the individual. No one other than the individual or a collaborating group can determine its content. It is offered as a gift to others. In this spirit, the giver should respect the rights and liberties of the recipient.

» **Communal Effort**: Our community values creative cooperation and collaboration. We strive to produce, promote and protect social networks, public spaces, works of art, and methods of communication that support such interaction.

» **Civic Responsibility**: We value civil society. Community members who organize events should assume responsibility for public welfare and endeavor to communicate civic responsibilities to participants. They must also assume responsibility for conducting events in accordance with local, state and federal laws.

» **Leaving No Trace**: Our community respects the environment. We are committed to leaving no physical trace of our activities wherever we gather. We clean up after ourselves and endeavor, whenever possible, to leave such places in a better state than when we found them.

» **Participation**: Our community is committed to a radically participatory ethic. We believe that transformative change, whether in the individual or in society, can occur only through the medium of deeply personal participation. We achieve being through doing. Everyone is invited to work. Everyone is invited to play. We make the world real through actions that open the heart.

» **Immediacy**: Immediate experience is, in many ways, the most important touchstone of value in our culture. We seek to overcome barriers that stand between us and a recognition of our inner selves, the reality of those around us, participation in society, and contact with a natural world exceeding human powers. No idea can substitute for direct experience.

Is it the individual or is it the system?

SYSTEMS ARISE FOR a reason, in response to something out of balance or as a response to some need. Individualism was a much-needed response to monarchy, repression and being locked into a caste or class system; it was intended as a means to empowerment and freedom. Healthy individualism is self-respecting and self-loving. However, our current iteration of individualism seems to be an extreme form. In American culture, we put so much emphasis on the achievements of the individual that some people actually believe in the possibility of being a "self-made man." Yet every act is dependent on a vast network of individuals, past and present. We are always the recipients of more good than we could ever give back.

While personal responsibility and personal freedom offer great things to us, there's a loneliness in our cultural inheritance: The dark side of individualism is isolation. It has tremendous costs in terms of mental health, healing, economies and exploitation. The conditions that occur at the extreme end of the spectrum of independence—social isolation, rejection, and disconnection—often lead to antisocial behavior; these conditions are common to all violent offenders, often from a very young age.

And yet despite its potential toxicity, the image of the lone heroic individual—whether it's cowboys, pioneers, superheroes or celebrities—remains a powerful one. It has deep roots in history and mythology (one lone visionary saves the world; a single superhero does more than entire army). We have been told over and over the story of the immigrant who came from nothing and made good by simply working harder or working smarter, no matter the structural forces arrayed against him. We may have needed this narrative at one point—it freed people and gave them agency. It is not inherently bad. But the cult of the individual puts a tremendous amount of pressure on a person to do everything for him or herself, not to rely on others or on the tribe.

The individual mythos is not only costly; it's false. Everyone who succeeds does so with some level of support of community structures, from the family to the federal government. We can be exceptional leaders or insightful inventors and iconoclastic artists, but we still owe the whole.

Conversely, we can do everything "right" as individuals and still we rise or fall to some degree with the collective. Anyone who has lived through a major economic cycle knows this: If I save, but a thousand other people don't, my ship still goes down. I pay my mortgage, but the financial markets go through a restructuring, and my house loses 50% of its value. The bond market stutters, and public workers are put on leave. I put my money in a pension fund that invests in Enron, and far-away bad actors leave me penniless. I have health care, but 35% of the population does not, so I bear the costs for everyone. If we are for peace, but our country goes to war, the bombs fall on our houses equally. Each of us, as an individual, can do everything seemingly right, but we still end up suffering. We are all inextricably connected.

Our ignorance of this connection is partly attributable to our inability to see the big picture. So much in our environment is happening at a scale that we just can't take in. Imagine the vast networks of people and communities to which we belong as a massive pointillist painting, the size of an IMAX screen. At a distance, this painting presents a cohesive image with patterns and shapes and lines. In our daily lives, however, we encounter only a few square inches. To us, it's just a series of individual and unconnected pixels. Seeing the "painting" this way isn't a failing; it just means we're human. Most of us (myself included) are focused on our own lives. Yet it's important to at least attempt to step back and see how those dots create something larger. Because whether we are aware of it or not, the big picture is still impacting us. Our limited perceptions can give us faulty information—I am responsible only to myself!—but we are not fated to stay in the illusion of disconnection. In our house we used to say that the kids were "great observers, bad concluders." They see everything, but they don't always draw the right conclusions from what they see. That's true of adults, too. We can cultivate our mental, emotional, perceptual and inter-personal skills to see differently, and to become better observers and better concluders.

No one is alone. We are all part of a connected universe—we are all points in a constellation we cannot get enough distance from to clearly see. That connection is always available to us, and, with practice, it gets easier and easier to access.

There are many ways to address disconnection. Some of them can be achieved at the individual level, as I found in my experience with yoga. It connected me more fully to myself and my immediate community. The systemic disconnection that is a result of the living structures, however, can be more effectively addressed at the community level.

How do we live together better?

DURING THE LAST several hundred years we have experienced intense and ongoing changes in the way we live together, and in the kinds of connection we have to our families, tribes, and neighborhoods—in essence, the shape and make-up of our communities has changed.

In my "talking to strangers" period, I could see that some of the people I engaged with had a real truth to speak. Even though they lived on the fringes, they were often there by choice. I wanted to know why they chose to live the way they did, what brought them there, and what kept them there.

This realization led me to explore some alternative kinds of communities as models for ways we might live together more successfully.

What I learned was that there are thousands of forms of community experimentation going on around the world, and ten times that number of people who are looking at ways of redesigning how we live together—in some cases, integrating wisdom from tribal communities with new technology. Some are ad hoc, while some are more organized—what people call "intentional communities."

Experiments in community

ONE NIGHT, UNDER a starry Pacific sky, in a hot springs bath canti-levered over the cliffs of Big Sur, I got into a lengthy conversation with a tall, dark-haired former Coca-Cola Marketing executive. She was a new empty nester who had left her job. She was temporarily on this stretch of coast, living in a fantastically painted and adorned old school bus, in between global travels. She had just returned from a visit to Damanhur, in the Italian Alps.

Damanhur, she told me, her high cheekbones and wide open enthusiastic eyes reflecting back the moonlight, was one of the oldest and most successful alternative communities on Earth. They anchored their community around a temple carved deep in the mountains. It was prosperous and stable and committed to experimenting and modeling a new way of constructing society. The two of us began to share what we knew of all such places, enumerating the other famous attempts at reinventing community: Findhorn in Scotland, Auro-ville in India, The Farm in Tennessee, and more. The conversation ignited within me a spark of intention to visit as many of these places as I could.

Over the ensuing years, in order to learn what might be imported into the general culture, I've sought out communities that have successfully sustained a base of operations and grown to the scale of small towns. All have sustained themselves at least thirty years while preserving some aspects of democratic consciousness or personal voice. I've visited the township of Auroville in India, founded in 1968, where the driving desire is spiritual harmony. I've traveled to ZEGG in Germany, founded more recently, with its focus on individual freedoms and conscious communication.

Every time I drop into a new culture and start this inquiry, it becomes clear that we're in choice: we can initiate, and attempt to craft, any kind of culture we would like to create. These communities show that there are many ways to live, people have and are crafting infinite variations of sharing resources and governance, managing joys and concerns,. The evolution of how we live together is always happening, someone is always pushing the edge.

The monks of Maulbronn

PEOPLE HAVE BEEN experimenting with alternative communities for thousands of years. We decided to go and look at a very old implementation of alternative community ans see what might be learned. My son Connor and I arrived in Maulbronn to see the monastery when the sky was already black-blue and the metal slats on the night jalousies were rolled down tight. Deserted streets, barely a car.

Next to the cloister's main arch was the Hotel zum Klosterpost, a central building with old-style *Fachwerk* and double-sided stone steps gracefully curving up to the door. I rang the night bell. I asked—in elegant high German, the formal kind used to balance out an inappropriate, unplanned late arrival and bad shoes—about a double room.

"*Haben Sie vielleicht eine Zimmer fur heute nacht? Ein doppel?*"

A male voice answered, "*Oh, Nein.*" Then there was a long pause.

"*Weil wir wolten die Kloster morgen besuchen,*" I said. We want to visit the cloister in the morning.

"*Ja, sind sie allein dar?*" Was it just me, he wanted to know.

"*Mein Sohn ist dabei.*" My son, I answered.

"*Ich komme gerade.*" I'm coming down.

In a few moments a tall, lanky guy with wide-open, deep eyes came around the corner from behind. He might have been 43. He was very interested in why I was there; a woman traveling with children in this tiny town at 10 at night, without a reservation, was a rarity.

The man was sexy in a middle-aged, I'm-interested-in-you kind of way, and his chatter didn't stop. He loved San Francisco, and mentioned friends in

Los Gatos. He was an engineer, and had studied and lived in Berlin. This was his family's place.

"My name is Juergen, I live two doors down, if you need anything." Did I? I momentarily imagined him naked, then struck the thought.

We waited at the front desk while he tried to figure out something that would work for us. Soon we had two rooms—one for me, and across the hall, a monk-like cell without a bath for my son.

Maybe it was the monks, or the interaction with Juergen, or the fact that things just seem to work out, but I liked the way the town felt.

Kloster Maulbronn was once a Cistercian monastery, founded in 1138 and occupied by Catholic monks almost continuously until the German state of Baden-Wurtemburg took it over. It became an Evangelical seminary in the early 1800s. Today it's a UNESCO World Heritage site, and is essentially physically (if not spiritually) intact.

The Cistercian order was initially formed in some part as a reaction to what some monks felt had become a path far too concerned with worldly affairs: Catholic monks owned property, and had become engaged in questions of trade. Though the monks of the order would address this situation by recommitting to a rejection of the secular world, Kloster Maulbronn was intended to be a movement not away from something, but toward something— toward restoring the primary focus of daily life on studying God in the world. This was achieved through a commitment to poverty, service, quiet simplicity and humility, all to better reflect Jesus' life.

There were monks and lay brothers in the cloister. They took the same vows and had the same focus, but for the most part lived and worked separately. The monks were educated; they read and wrote and studied and interpreted and taught the scriptures. Inside the inner courtyards of Maulbronn, the monks woke before sunrise and were for prayers called seven times during the day. These prayers structured their days.

Everything about the interior architecture of Maulbronn reinforced the order's vows and beliefs. Unlike many castles, cathedrals and churches of the era, as a gesture of humility, the cloister had no high towers. The monks stood the entire time they prayed in small, booth-like separated spaces— together but alone. Unless it was urgent they didn't speak, but kept their ears open to listen and distill what was important. They used sign language for communicating with each other regarding daily affairs. They ate two meals a day, lunch and dinner, and on holy days only dinner. They ate no meat, but drank red wine with each meal.

The lay brothers led a similar life within the walled community of the monastery, though they did not enter the actual study halls and prayer rooms of the cloister. They had equivalent accommodations, a dining hall and a shared kitchen, but did not interact with the monks. During mass, the lay brothers were separated by a wall. They vowed to the same focus on God and were usually highly skilled tradesman, such as carpenters and bakers, who did their work as a service. Traditionally, Cistercians worked the land. This order was highly skilled in water management, and had enacted amazing feats of engineering.

Medieval monks and the generations of monks that followed had worked this land with sophistication and foresight. They made a conscious choice to design their life and community in a way that supported their deepest intentions and values. It's no different now. The monks could have made the choice to simply accept the status quo of that era, but they didn't: they chose to redesign and innovate.

The desire for change that led the Cistercians to form a new sect in the eleventh century is the same impulse that drives people to form intentional communities today. This process has been going on forever—things get out of balance and some minority sees it and begins to rethink it, and slowly bits of that thinking transfer to the collective. In the transference period, however, there is a lot of unnecessary suffering and malaise among the people living in the imbalanced status quo. To shorten that suffering, we can all be trying to redesign as we go—we can be in constant evaluation and growth.

✳

Idealism in India

ON THE OTHER side of the world, there is a completely different experiment going on. The community of Auroville asks "How do we bring people from all over the world together in harmony and prosperity?" It is for those who, in the words of its cofounder, known as The Mother, are "people of goodwill.... All those who thirst for progress and aspire to a higher and truer life."

In mid January of 2013, the hot and dry season, after a week of working with our development team in Mumbai and Pune, I headed to Auroville.

I took a car from the Sparsa Tiruvanamalai airport, rode through the stunning Tamil countryside of mountains and palms and rice paddies to Auroville. Despite the ready availability of Google images, I'd expected Auroville to be an organized, gated community. But like all of southeast India, nothing was as expected.

Spread over a wide swath of land, settler villages were interspersed with native villages. The town contained the usual colorful chaos of India: motorbikes loaded with unimaginable volumes of goods, sacred cows standing in the middle of the street, sari-draped girls with flowers in their hair walking in clusters down the road, palm trees swaying over tiny trash fires, plastic debris scattered everywhere.

Auroville was founded in the late 1960s by Sri Aurobindo, an Indian yogi, and his western partner, known as "The Mother." It is a utopian community. When I arrived, I was taken down a series of funky dirt roads to a private home, dotted with children's toys and signs of daily living. A guest room was waiting for me. I had a sparse but comfortable single bed, a desk and a deck for my yoga. Perfectly fine, especially after resort living, and it was only 500 rupees (about seven dollars) a night.

Auroville is organized in self-contained theme camps, which all have guesthouses. On arriving, I walked to the camp next door to register myself. There was a vibrant blond woman in a news cap named Wiebke. She was German, from Berlin, and had lived in Auroville on and off for five years. Her career in Germany was social enterprise; her job at Auroville was to further its master plan and visioning process. Wiebke and I spoke in a mixture of German, English, and yoga-speak.

As we were walking away, Selveraj—a friend of a friend I was meant to connect with later in the week—drove up and introduced himself. He invited us both for tea. I climbed on Wiebke's scooter, and away we went into the warm unlit Tamil evening.

Selveraj's house had big carved doors, an expansive wraparound porch and thick pillars and columns. Inside, the center atrium was surrounded by lounging areas and littered with simple terracotta pots and metal pans, old wood furniture and instruments, all in slight sweet wabi-sabi disarray. Selveraj prepared tea with hot milk for the three of us, and then we talked.

Selveraj was born in Auroville, and remembers The Mother. He now runs a high school and a guesthouse, and managed other things. He was, in short, an insider's insider. The conversation between him and Wiebke ran the length and breadth of online learning, educational philosophies, children, change, even TED talks. Whereas she saw the conflicts and obstacles and problems and class issues in Auroville, Selveraj saw the vision.

Afterwards, I got on the back of Wiebke's motorcycle, and away we went. I couldn't have found the shared campus at the heart of Auroville on my own, and it definitely wasn't walkable—but the best part about riding with this stranger was that everywhere we stopped, she knew everyone.

We went out for pizza; it was the first time in a month that I didn't eat curry. Wiebke's friends were social entrepreneurs, people she knew when she ran a prominent shared workspace in Berlin. They were French, Australian, American, Indian. Some ran similar entrepreneurial centers in Bombay and Pondicherry, and were full of ideas.

No one seemed to drink, though it was the kind of dinner that, back home, would have been fueled by wine and whiskey. Ideas were discussed with energy and fluidity, and impromptu plans were made in the heat of discussion. The Assistant Director for the movie *Life of Pi*, Seran, came over to say hello to Wiebke. He told her he was casting extras for another film, and wanted to know if she would like a spot. Soon, we were all making plans for a Conscious Capitalism Simulcast and looking at the Eco-Femme site, and talking about the personal characteristics to get things done right. It was many hours and several lime sodas later when I got back to my room. This is an international community, where the mobile can drop in and out and feel right at home.

The next morning, I awakened to the distant sound of flag-raising cere-monies for Republic Day. I walked to the road and found breakfast. Auroville's sprawling layout was difficult to navigate without a scooter, which I didn't have, so I found a driver. Narayanraj was twenty-eight and spoke nine Indian dialects. He became my guide and escort; I saw him on and off every day.

I started my day in the Auroville visitor center, where I picked up a slew of pamphlets and books on the Mother. I saw the Matrimandir, a giant golden dome that is the spiritual heart of the city, from the outside. The Matrimandir looks like a big golfball. It's a meditation space and temple, with concentration room and the 13 separate chambers. I walked and walked all over, visiting many of the theme camps and getting a feeling for the place.

There was something good at Auroville. Something still hopeful— Sustainable, organic and green. On the other hand, it felt like the world was passing it by in some ways. For example, they seemed to be still debating garbage management, when many of the cities around the world had already figured that out. I attended a half dozen community meetings focused on specific topics related to managing or planning the future of Auroville. There was a lot of processing, a lot of conversation, and very little seemed to get accomplished. Group management and problem solving seemed to exacerbate the drama of human systems, and lead to long winded, paralyzing attempts at decision making.

Auroville was fantastic, I would love to go back; yet the community didn't offer a model for governance that I thought could be replicated and brought home. I guess we learn as much from what doesn't work as from what does.

I returned from India not discouraged but even more curious about the other groups of people out there in the world experimenting with ways of being together.

Talking to plants in Germany

A YEAR LATER, my son Connor and I again went in search of people expanding the definition of living in community. This time, we traveled to Germany to visit ZEGG, the Center for Experimental Community Design. We were familiar with the basics about ZEGG: we knew that it was an intentional community where they strive to make transparency, self-awareness, love, trust and compassionate honesty the new cultural norms. The people there hold this to be true: "We believe that it takes a village to raise a consciousness. We intend that our work and play together will be transformative not only for small communities, but for the community of the world as well."

One of the hallmarks of ZEGG is that is has developed and codified a communication approach called "ZEGG Forum" that they have practiced for the last 50 years. Their methodology has been taken forward across the world, and today there are ZEGG Forum practice groups in many cities. Their work, based on truth-telling and transparency, is about expressing an individual experience within a committed group. There is a strong Nonviolent Communication (NVC) component in their communications, which also include a great deal of ritualized play.

ZEGG is an hour outside of Berlin, and we drove through black sky summer thunderstorms and hail. As we approached ZEGG, however, down a long two-lane highway, the sun came out, a luminous clarity suffusing the fields and trees.

Our arrival, unintentionally, coincided with the beginning of a three-day event that brings together the global leadership of ecovillages and intentional communities from 3 continents—and those that are looking for better ways to

149

organize. Because it was a learning event, there were pavilions and workshops on a wide variety of topics, ranging from solar power to food workshops to managing relationships with local conventional communities.

One of the workshops was on practicing ESP—with people, animals *and plants*. I had never even *heard* of plant telepathy practice. First, we paired up and tried some exercises designed to elicit ESP skills from people. For example, we were asked to imagine a color and transmit it to our partner. My assigned partner saw the green of sun coming through those rain soaked leaves—exactly the image had I pictured in my mind and invited her to "read." She sent me a snowball. I caught that in return.

The next assignment was to find a plant, and talk to it. I was truly skeptical, but being game for anything, I put my heart into it. I found a spot near a lovely, leafing-out tree, sat down beside it, and dropped into meditation. When my heartbeat and breathing felt synchronized, I followed the suggested protocol, which was to first ask permission to converse by telepathing to the tree a simple question: "Hi, can we communicate?"

After receiving a feeling of agreement, I asked the tree what its life was like. What did the tree want to show me? What ensued was a powerful visual: Instantly, the green field I was sitting in turned to stark snow, and I felt a rapid inward pull, to the center and deep underground, about four or five feet into the earth; a sensation of being curled up into a warm ball. This was followed by huge exhale, with a mandate to grow and grow and grow as fast as possible, followed again by a slowing down as the growth met resistance and the winter came on again. The tree showed me in rapid perception the progression and sensation of its annual life cycle, a huge oscillation in force, in contraction and expansion. It was very fast but incredibly vivid.

During the growth phase, I felt that the tree was encountering a limitation to growth; a sort of "pain" on the south side of its trunk. When I emerged from the exercise, I looked at the trunk's south face: It was bound to a stake to stop it from growing into the kitchen area pathway.

The tree-talk made me aware of the life and activity around me that I don't notice in day-to-day life. But plants, like people, are all different. Connor tried to talk to a weedy flower, but when he asked it to communicate, said that the plant told him to "fuck off."

Our experience at ZEGG, however, wasn't limited to extraordinary methods. We were also able to explore more practical ways to strengthen our ability to relate and connect to others.

In our short time there, we learned how Nonviolent Communication is put into practice in the community. NVC, as it is called, is an approach to conflict resolution founded by psychologist Marshall Rosenberg. It's a foundational element of communication and problem-solving in many intentional communities—but it's not just for people attempting to remake how we live together. The technique is practiced by people in many walks of life, and is a common form of intervention in diplomacy and law enforcement situations.

Practitioners of NVC believe that all conflict comes from unmet needs, so the work begins with being able to recognize one's own needs and hear the needs of others. Once you can identify and describe those unmet needs and communicate around them, you can find a resolution. While this may seem simplistic, the NVC method has been used in war torn environments from Rwanda to Northern Ireland to initiate peace and connection even in extreme circumstances.

When a community member at ZEGG experiences a personal trigger or an conflict, the member can express it in a ZEGG forum. The forum can be of any size, the ones I've attended have had about 40 people in the circle. Within a safe container, people stand to share or explore what is happening for them. Participants in the forum observe and support the initiating member, offering feedback on what is expressed in the form of mirrors. The forum is not limited to speech; it involves movement and voice and excitement. A person is free to act out emotions, to embody emotions if he or she can't find the words.

This is the place from which these people are working. If you want to build a building, talk to the plants and the animals. Tell them what's going on, and ask them to please make way. If you want to cohabit with spiders, speak with them and make an agreement. If you want to know something, just ask.

Consensus on the Dutch Coast

ONE SUMMER AFTER a work trip to Amsterdam, I traveled to the Netherlands.

There's a high wind blowing in off the Atlantic, caressing the big dunes and sweeping across the sea level landscape. The wind grazes orderly homes with red tiled roofs, symmetrical shutters, stark graphic decoration, clean windows. Dozens of self-contained blondines on bicycles head by, everyone so healthy and so serious. The children, in contrast to their elders, holler and tear up the place. Only when drinking do Dutch adults seem to let go of their self-containment.

People come out to this sparse Atlantic Coast to live simply, to swim in the ocean, to eat fresh mussels in season and then return to their office jobs having vacationed with their families, refreshed. It's a family place but I'm here alone, looking for one particular non-tourist: Branca Prins, the foremost scholar of Dutch culture, who despite his public warnings of the dire consequences of climate change has moved ever and ever closer to the edge of the continent, to an island almost in the North Sea. If his entire country goes underwater, he will go first.

Prins was maybe 70 years old, very fit and handsome. I've made this trek to pick his brain on why Dutch culture has emerged with such apparent tolerance, with such a live-and-let live attitude on everything from sexuality to drugs, even alongside this culture of self-contained individuals. How does the moderate socialist center hold yet also support what is clearly thriving commercialism? What aspect of belief or culture enables it? What is it based on?

People have attempted varying forms of governing-by-community for a long time. Even representative democracy in the United States is intended to be governing by community; but it has gotten so far away from direct control between the electorate and the elected that it does not really work. In some countries, though, the model of governance for thousands of years has been based on agreement and collectivism that we have never experienced in the United States. The Dutch Polder Model is one example.

Prins invites me in, with a nod and a huge smile, his massive hands holding the door. Over strong coffee, amidst the artifacts of his well-traveled and curious life, Prins begins to explain the model in which the Dutch thrive.

Sitting back in a worn tweed armchair, Prins began to explain.

"The Dutch, you see, live in a constant dance with the land. Starting in the eleventh century, Dutch engineers began draining wetlands and fen. For hundreds of years, they have relied on a complex system of locks and dams to prevent their fields from flooding. Those reclaimed lands are known as *polders*."

He continued, "The Polder Model of governance is thought to have arisen in the Middle Ages, out of an approach to land management executed with the idea that a people cannot be separated from the place or the land they occupy. But keeping polder land arable required an elaborate system of dikes, dams, and canals and constant maintenance. The level of cooperation required to manage the land through a fully functioning dike system was high; there had to be complete agreement on every aspect. If one neighbor failed to do his part, all were at risk. The penalty for failing to cooperate in maintaining the system was the very real: the drowning of land, creatures and entire villages."

There was a long pause as we looked out the window and I let this idea sink in. I asked Prins, "So do you think it is enlightened self-interest that makes people more prone to collaborate?"

Prins nodded, "Sure. In Dutch culture, there is a long history of cooperation for the greater good—even when there are significant differences in opinion. Cooperation is not based on some noble ideal, but on a deep pragmatism; for thousands of years, the Dutch have needed complete agreement on just who was manning which pumping station, monitoring which dike, simply to live on their land."

"That's pretty impressive." I said.

"BUT, that doesn't mean it's easy!" he replied. "More recently, the Polder Model was extended to governance in a concerted effort to rise above partisanship for the greater good. This model was first extended to governance just after the Second World War, when the Netherlands was rebuilt swiftly with the cooperation of all political parties and labor unions; a true coalition of rivals. They had to have unanimous consent in order to pass any piece of legislation, and at that time, perhaps out of the urgency to rebuild from destruction, the cooperative model succeeded."

The model was used again in the late 1980s, a period of impressive economic expansion sometimes referred to as the "Dutch Miracle." During this time legislation moved very slowly—but once a decision was made, there was no resistance or hidden agendas in implementation. It's not clear that this model, based on the pace and structure required for the physical management of land (which is slow and detailed) can be effectively translated to a modern, fast-moving economy and government. Listening to everyone's views takes a long time; consideration is a patient art."

I considered this in the context of the pressure to decide; in my culture *"perfect is the enemy of good"* is a common slogan. I said, "That seems out of step with the current pace of life, in a world where decisions move at a microclick, and the global modus operandi is to ask forgiveness, not permission."

Prins replied, "Well that's not necessarily a good thing. Innovation in technology and science are moving faster than a shared social compact on their use can be developed. As the world sped up and a global economic culture began to dominate, even the Dutch themselves began to push back on the Polder model: it was in fact too slow to keep up with world's intertwined "progress." The Dutch governing bodies began to resemble those of many other squabbling senates and houses of representatives. I can't help but wonder how long it will take for the pendulum to swing back."

"Yes," I agreed, "after all, people who aren't part of the decision, who aren't brought into the fold, often hold on to resistance and resentment and cause problems later on. I suppose this repressed dissonance or disagreement may show up in time."

When institutions disconnect us

INSTITUTIONS CAN ONLY shift in micro increments. Most of the institutions in our lives—education, justice, government, work, religion—are far-reaching and deeply entrenched. It's difficult, if not impossible, to effect radical change overnight. After all, that's not how entrenchment happened; that, too, was a long process that took decades, centuries, even millennia. Institutions are created in a certain context—of place, of time, of need. They start with a purpose, then a story and a way of being or working is developed. This narrative is encoded as "belief" or "creed" or "policy" or "standards," and from that moment on, things begin to ossify. In the process of becoming "institutionalized," all kinds of parallel systems arise to support the main institution. Individuals and companies begin to bet their livelihoods and identities on the way things are; they are rewarded for maintaining the status quo.

But the world around our institutions is not static. Intractable institutions generally cease to serve us, no matter how effective or well-intentioned they may have been at one point. They can become a block to positive change. And the more the context around institutions changes, the more of a drag or a drain they can become. I keep an ongoing list called "little tiny bullshits," small ways in which bureaucracies create unnecessary frictions between common sense and reality.

Education is another example. The context of education has changed—the Internet has made individualized learning assessments and teaching programs cost effective—yet the public education system we grew up with still continue essentially unchanged, teaching a 19th century curriculum and process.

Where does knowledge live now? What is a credential? How are skills and mastery really measured now? What does NOW need, or better yet, what will the future need? The ship of public education always seems years behind the times.

Breaking out of a system that has its own inertia is not easy. The longer the institution has been around, and the more people and resources are tied to its culture, the harder it is. Think of it as a tree: a young sapling is relatively easy to transplant, but moving a grown tree means moving its deeply embedded root system—often breaking open the pavement or ground and uprooting nearby plants to do so.

So it is with changing systems that are embedded. Even when they are sick, obstructive or inefficient, it can take a lot of force to uproot them. It's a delicate skill to do it right, without causing collateral damage. Take the closing of a military base, for example. Even if you're convinced that we need to decrease spending in that sector, you can't just close a base without thinking about the people who are directly or indirectly dependent on it. From the personnel and their families to the local businesses that serve them, a broad population may be devastated by the attempt to "fix" an institution without a plan for what will replace it.

One sign that an institution has become calcified is when its values and approaches create more separation, disconnection, or exclusion from the human family. Systems that tear us apart from one another are wrong. But how do we redesign these broken, or at the least suboptimal, systems? How do we ensure that our institutions are learning and growing machines, promoting inclusion and connection? How can we revitalize and reinvigorate things that are working?

As things stand, the dominant approach to community in the West— the unofficial institution that guides our choices about how we live with others— is propelled by a century-long shift away from communal living. The result, as we've discussed, is isolation, loneliness and disconnection. But we don't have to accept this system; we can question it, open ourselves to inquiry and experimentation.

One of my least favorite sayings is, "It is what it is." It's shortsighted, passive and powerless. On the other hand if we can say "This is what I value, and what we together value," then we—like the Maulbronn monks, the residents of Auroville and ZEGG, and the practitioners of the Polder Model—can orient our lives toward the intention of community and connection. We build our common spaces to serve this intention. We create our governance and workflow to serve this intention. We learn to communicate with each other in a way that honors this intention.

We do not have to escape into the wilderness to implement change. We can find community in an urban group house, a farm, or a retreat. An intentional community can occur in a suburban area, where people consciously buy a pod of houses in the same two or three block radius and create their own family shire. It can be a group of people who focus on a single issue—spirituality, eco-consciousness, artistic expression—and approach that issue holistically within the constructs of existing communities. Any human living with other humans can use conscious communication techniques like NVC and benefit, at work, play, or home. Because conscious communication is about connecting—and using connection to solve problems.

Whether in an intentional community, a co-housing arrangement or a monastery, such experiments in living together seem to be rooted in an overarching desire to achieve a more peaceful, harmonious existence. People are asking and answering questions about the way we share our space, and actively choosing to create meaningful communities based on shared values. We can redesign community in the very space we occupy, and around the topics that matter the most to us. If we do, those changes will ripple outward—one degree at a time.

Do try this at home

FOR MANY YEARS, I created gatherings and hosted people in the interest of creating community. I curated dozens of events, from 100 to 2000 people, to bring people together. I hosted book signings and poetry slams. For two years, I along with a friend and work partner, hosted weekly vegetarian suppers in an old Victorian in downtown San Francisco, in a community we named LoveSpring. Each week, we had live music, meditation and a guest speaker talking on some aspect of self-development, service work, creativity or adventure. About 400 joined, with a solid core of weekly regulars.

That's continued to evolve into new forms. I'm experimenting now with creating a little bit of a shared living space in my own house. We call it Casa Cantando, or the singing house. People come in and out. I am totally happy for them to come. There is always a room or a bed for them. Some stay for a few weeks when they are between houses, and some have stayed months. There are always visitors; someone new is always at the table, bringing their stories and discoveries to share.

After varying degrees of urban and suburban living, being a pretty traditional householder, living in a single family home where both parents and the kids were in the same house, this experiment in communal living was a big departure. My original expectation of a traditional life wasn't going to pan out. Maybe post-child rearing I could have rented a little studio or something—but I didn't. I found a larger place, with one side tucked into a mountain and the other leaning out over the hill. A great wall of windows looks out on the San Francisco Bay.

I didn't really see the group thing coming. Initially, I just had a lot of guests. People would come for a week or two, or even a few months. But over time it morphed into a community. The people here now are all adults, living consciously, in choice and collaboration. There are always people to talk to. There is music, people making beautiful things and cooking shared meals. Tonight's dinner, by one resident scholar, was a turnip, ginger and squash soup. One of the guys has transformed the fireplace into an altar of sorts: a focal point for memory, aspiration, and devotion. We make music; do our practices, eat, talk, watch movies.

There are complexities and imperfections. The people who have stayed are compatible and easy to deal with. Is that by design? And I'm kind of in charge, so am I really sharing my space? Am I sharing equally, or are people just staying here by my allowance?

So while Casa Cantando is a rich way to live and love, it is also imbalanced. It isn't yet designed in a way that is sustainable for an entire collective. I bear the bulk of the costs and the bulk of the maintenance. At the moment, two other people are living here. One is contributing cash, probably at 60% of the market rate. The other isn't contributing cash, but is contributing in other ways. But then again, if she *was* paying, we would lose some flexibility. There is a benefit to not having formal members, or shared governance, but rather this looser arrangement of sharing the space. If the arrangement were completely balanced, we might split the expenses differently, and the work. So, it's is a work-in-progress, but something here is turning into more than an experiment. This is a new way of life for me: to live communally, coexisting within a sharing economy. And it is probably going to continue to become *more* communal, not less.

I'm not the only one engaged in this exploration. Another wave of intentional communities is currently taking hold. Over the last decade, the number of known intentional communities has grown from five or six hundred to tens of thousands. There's also been an explosion in what's called cooperative housing, an emerging model of living together. It started in the Benelux countries and now has outposts in many urban areas in the United States. It's a response both to rising housing costs and to dissatisfaction with the isolation of traditional living structures.

In the San Francisco Bay area alone, there are dozens of adult "tech ashrams" and group houses, in which people cohabitate in giant Victorian era houses. Each person gets a bedroom and a bath, private or shared. Members share expenses, and they share the public spaces. In some of these communities, the members have rotating food duties; others hire a chef for the house. There's always something happening. Some residents stay a year, some stay for decades.

Trying a change in lifestyle impacts the people in my life, especially my children. They grew up in traditional suburban households, in Chicago and California. They grew up with Nutella crepes and Honey Nut Cheerios. Now, we've eliminated packaged foods in the house. Everything is in mason jars: dried fruits, nuts, grains. We keep basic staples and supplements. We make our own kombucha. It's a different way of being. The kids think that living this way is a little off the mainstream and that, on some level, my housemates are intruders.

I think my sons are confronting their own prejudices about ownership and control. With my daughter, it is very different. She comes with her baby, and we put the crib in my room and we sleep together and we cuddle up and everything is amazing.

Parents often talk about what it is like to help their children grow, but it is worth recognizing that, as parents, we aren't static either. We experience transitions in our institutions, economies, communities, our intimate relationships, and we evolve. So while there is not necessarily a clash between the old way and the new, this communal living arrangement might push my children to allow *me* to change. My kids seem comfortable with not clinging to their nostalgia or keeping me in a mental box. They know that the mandate of a tree is to grow, and so it is with humans. We want to keep growing and changing for the rest of our lives. We can't get hung up on the way keeping things the way they are.

For me, the sharing is not about money, although it certainly *could* be about money and there would be no shame in that. On a purely economic basis, if I am going to take responsibility for my existence into old age, I cannot live at the level my kids remember from their childhoods. I cannot even live in the same neighborhood that I provided to them, if I'm to self-fund for

40 more years: I have to live in a more conscious way, and that may mean sharing space, or exploring alternative ways of caring for myself as I age. Many people I've encountered feel, as I do, that we will likely have to work outside the system to meet our needs—physically, mentally and spiritually. The systems and institutions in which we live don't have our backs. Most people in the US are three to six weeks away from being broke. They keep steady on a month-to-month income, but barely. For many people, homelessness is just a string of bad luck away.

Earlier this year, I got an email from a friend—let's call him Nate—who was down on his luck.

"I have nowhere to turn right now," Nate wrote. "Last summer, I had $17,000 in savings. But I took some hits this summer, and now I'm at zero. There were health issues and legal issues with my ex, and then somebody bought the company I licensed my truck from. The new owner took my truck, and assigned it to his brother. For two months, I didn't have any income. I got behind on my rent... Last week, after seven years as a reliable tenant, the landlord evicted me. I have nowhere to turn. Can you help?"

I called my friend Colin, and I told him the story. Nate had been a single dad for a decade, taking sole care of his daughter. Colin immediately asked what the friend's rent was. I said $1,800. He said, "Okay, well let's each do half. He'll have rent for this month—but how will he get caught up?" We were stumped. I posted a notice about Nate on Facebook. I kept his case anonymous, but described the kind of person he was and the bind he was in. I asked if, as a community, we could help. Some sent 100 dollars, some sent ten. Within seventy-two hours we had raised $4,100, I sent him these deposits with Square cash.

Nate thinks we saved his life, but really, we just came together and exercised our role as a community. More than that: As a community, we made a change in our trajectory. Maybe it wasn't even a full degree, but it was one small shift, a tiny puncture in the economic system. Everyone involved was changed because of that exchange. There was an instinctual response of love and connection, and it wasn't about money. It was about open heartedness, and interdependence. It was about an online community, helping in the real world. But what a strange world Nate had lived in, alone up until the point of asking, not knowing if the world would be there for him and his daughter.

Yet even with all of my openness, all of my research and exploration, living differently isn't easy. I may have witnessed conflict resolution using NVC in ZEGG, but when it comes time to address conflict in the context of my own experiment, I still feel bad bringing it up. For instance, one of the guys at Casa Cantando has a taste for whiskey. One evening I had a dinner party, and wanted to be able to offer my guests a drink, so I bought a bottle in advance. When I got home, the whiskey was gone. In a moment of frustration, instead of talking about it, I put a Post-It note up on the walls. "The following are *not* for sharing: Green drinks, alcohol, or single serving beverages of any type." Conscious communication is key, but I basically fell back on Post-It notes. How unskillful is that? The pace of communication for resource sharing requires time and practice.

Later, I met someone who told me that it's not enough for a community or family to have an *idea*: They have to have a shared language, and body of shared knowledge, in order to even talk about the issues that arise. We have to live and practice the ideals we hold. It's the only way they are tested and refined.

Most intentional communities aim to build a successful culture and community based on connection, ease, and some form of expanded aware-ness. These communities start with an idea: *We are going to see if a new way of being is possible in one or more dimensions.* In rethinking community, they engage in inquiry around design: What are our values? How do we govern ourselves? How do we collectively choose how to use and share resources of time, goods, money and services? Is there a spiritual base, or are we just cool people living together? What kind of housing is best? What blend of public and private will work best? Who will we invite to live with us? How will we conduct meals or determine who to dine with? How will we reach out to other people on a daily basis? How do we join and/or remove ourselves from the umbrella of the community?

Intentional communities are not cults; they are not communities where a charismatic leader takes advantage of residents to aggrandize his or her own status. They don't separate people from their loved ones and extended family, but invite them in.

The best intentional communities are also learning machines, and as with any experiment, there are sometimes mistakes. But in the successful examples, course correction is built into the design. If the community veers right and then veers left, the hope is that it gets tighter with each correction until they are more or less on course, and future course corrections are less drastic. Most intentional communities try a lot of strategies and solutions; some go off track, but to succeed, they wiggle into a groove.

Intentional communities start with a philosophy or a belief system—the grounding principles that help members keep a pole star. They have a commonly held worldview or set of values. Some are based on ecological living, some on art and ideas. Some are based on living out the idea that they're in the unity of all things, that all life is interconnected by a pervasive unifying force.

Beyond those grounding principles, principles of communication are foundational to the success of such communities. All successful intentional communities have a form of conscious communication practice, problem solving methodology, or conflict resolution practice. They have made sure that the group has the vocabulary, skills, tools, and processes to get in touch with their own emotions and feelings, to be able to express their needs, and to listen to others. These communities invest much time and attention in interpersonal communications. They usually try to clear conflicts as they arise, rather than letting problems grow until they're too entrenched to be easily remedied. This would be valuable in any group.

Redesigning the way we live in our most personal spaces—in our homes, and communities—is the first, most immediately controllable place to begin. And it's all based on close relationships, which occupy a very special place between doing inner work, and meeting the big world.

THE HOUSE OF THE HEART

THE THIRD BODY

A man and a woman sit near each other, and they do not long
At this moment to be older, or younger, or born
In any other nation, or any other time, or any other place.
They are content to be where they are, talking or not talking.
Their breaths together feed someone whom we do not know.
The man sees the way his fingers move;
He sees her hands close around a book she hands to him.
They obey a third body that they share in common.
They have promised to love that body.
Age may come; parting may come; death will come!
A man and a woman sit near each other;
As they breathe they feed someone we do not know,
Someone we know of, whom we have never seen.
— ROBERT BLY

Love without fear

THE REALM OF romantic love, the source of merging and delight, also causes so much hiding, pain, and suffering. We lay so many expectations at the feet of the other—from "you complete me" to "until death do us part"—that when those expectations and agreements aren't met and we don't get the story we want to have, it brings our own unhealed things into high relief. Even if we've done work around that old pain or explored more connected, loving modes of being, the pair, or the dyad, seems the hardest place to hold onto newly acquired spiritual or psycho-emotional insights and skills. This topic is placed at the end of the book consciously: to me this is the most difficult and rewarding place to do the work of awakening.

Often, we put undue pressure onto partnership—trying to get the love we didn't get as children, filling holes in ourselves, trying to be each other's everything—rather than coming in as two strong beings in joy and clarity. Partnership is about choosing to be together, in the right balance between selective compromise and self-assertion. Sometimes the dyad is merely an arrangement: You make the children, I'll make the money. We have sex, we share the expenses. You praise me, I'll comfort you. But a true relationship is much deeper than an arrangement. It is an invitation for authenticity between two people, an invitation to help each other grow.

I'm writing this section for people who want to grow in their relationship with themselves and others, not just for those who want to upgrade "the arrangement." When it's really right, there's sense of two divinities (regardless of gender) merging into one.

Love at first sight

A FEW YEARS after Sean and I split up, I fell hard in love with a man on a plane to Albany, New York. It happened in a glance, in an instant. We talked the whole flight, and played with rocket ships and pocket toys to make his kids laugh. It was goofy and wonderful. At baggage claim, his daughter rode around on the carousel while we talked.

"Man, it is so clear how much you love your kids," I commented. He said quietly that being a good father was absolutely vital to him. In a sort of throwaway line, I said, "Well, you give what you need."

He stopped in his tracks and stared at me for a minute, then started talking about his own father and what he needed and didn't get. The conclusion of the conversation was this: "I needed it bad," he said. "I needed a good father badly, so that is exactly what I am trying to do."

We got together, sometimes in California where he lived, and sometimes in Chicago, where I lived. I fell in love with California's geography under his well-informed tutelage. We explored every corner of the state, up and down, from the Salton Sea to the Marble Mountains. Once we spent five days on the road, camping along the way, exploring esoteric places, like Slab City, an abandoned marine training base that had been transformed into an outpost for artists and eccentrics, a post-apocalyptic RV park for people on America's fringe.

He knew about birding and taught me what a *life list* is: *all the birds you have ever seen* noted in a single place. I taught him about art and myth and offered extensive super-dorky tech-tips, like what "http://" meant, how the Internet worked, and how simple it was to write code. He was a black belt in karate, and I brought him yoga. We were hyperverbal, reverent and irreverent. We hiked the soaked spring trails and broke beds in every city we visited. It was intoxicating. One day, we sat in a straddled embrace and looked into each others' pupils, and our bodies disappeared: the universe was in there, swirling and infinite. We laughed with our whole beings to be let in on this cosmic joke—inside as in out, we are swirling in the dust and molecules.

I loved his daughters, he loved my family. In a matter of months we were having Thanksgiving together, our blended families reenacting Pilgrims and Indians in costume. He proposed the following summer, on one knee, naked in a Sonoma stream: "Take me as I am."

Two years after we met, I moved to California. We married in July in an intimate ceremony under the waterfalls of Yosemite. My oldest son, Jarrett, broke into the ceremony midstream and did a sibling marriage ritual, in which our six kids stepped up to accept one another as brothers and sisters.

Instead of a honeymoon, we had a "fullmoon"—a log cabin in the park, dropping into cold mountain plunge pools, clambering over boulders, playing charades—with the eight of us making our new family. Then we settled in a house in Sonoma County. It was way too small for all of us but in the heart of wine country, where we'd expand the rose garden in the months following the wedding. We were organized and thoughtful, and the living together was simple and easy: pour-over single dose coffee and one dish suppers, long walks, great music, good work.

In those early days, I was commuting back to Chicago from Sunday until Friday. In that time apart, things that had been secrets during our courtship remained secrets. I did, however, begin to notice some troubling patterns in our relationship. One of the most difficult things for me to discover was that his word had little weight. A promise was subject to change, and an assertion was often a test balloon to see how others would react. At the time I wrote off these issues as minor bumps in the road, but I couldn't quite dismiss them altogether.

If I had been clear-headed and had known what I know today about healthy relationships, I may have been less complacent. The first or second time he broke an agreement with me I might have said, "Hmmm." By the third time, that healthier me would have tapped myself on the shoulder and said, "This person doesn't keep his agreements. You can save yourself a lot of heartache by moving on." But I didn't. There was too much entanglement by the time things became clear.

Before John and I reached our first anniversary, my father died. My dad, who had raised my brother and me, mellowed and grew into his full heart over the years, and stepped into love for my kids, was overtaken by cancer. After his funeral, I fell into a deep and quiet space. This coincided with starting to headhunt a replacement CEO for my company. I took a break to reset. I wrote, taught yoga, grieved, and watched everything about my career and life goals shift. During that time I wanted to just be *married*, to enjoy my partner, my beloved.

John's girls and my youngest son were the only ones still at home. All three were clear-headed, healthy, smart and shiny beings. As in many families, kids have mixed loyalties, confusions about what broke up their birth families, and a longing for those familiar days. With the girls, I was doing maintenance mom stuff: homework, cooking, chores, supplies—but without the cuddles and laughter and freedom and appreciation and pure love that grow between a parent and a child over many years together. I would show up for the school plays and soccer games and graduations, but in a strange third wheel situation: The girls' mother, John's ex, was also there, and John would get antsy and distant, sitting between the two of us. We would *try* to be like a family, but I felt an uncomfortable edge of not being wanted; of being an intruder. My son was resentful about the move and trying to adapt to the new situation. Plus, there were five cats, two dogs, and a Russian tortoise to contend with.

Sometimes, even with a lot of love, people can't face facts, devise a solution, and act together. That was our situation. There were money issues, there were work intensities, there were romantic interlopers. It was all so unnecessarily complicated.

We ground through it and eventually took care of all the messes and hang-overs—financial and relational. John's ex-wife and I started communicating, becoming allies and collaborators. I started doing some advisory work, and began to attract good, solid work in California; my business started growing. Things were in flow. I thought we'd gotten through the worst of it.

I was wrong.

Family of blood, choice and circumstance

IMAGINE US ALL: *My family of blood, choice and circumstance has gathered. Blow up beds, backpacks, and the debris of a dozen displaced people exploded across our minimalist space, clashing with the books into an appealing sort of chaos. There are life forms everywhere I look, in various states of activity and repose.*

Thanksgiving is tomorrow. The late afternoon light refracts off of damp green hills. There's a fire going, candles. In the kitchen, Jarrett, 27, is giving ten-year-old Grace a sous chef lesson, focused on knife care and handling. The two of them, the eldest and the youngest, have excavated their favorite recipes. Today they will make a hazelnut tart, cranberry relish, fennel-sausage-sage stuffing, and a rich squash and pumpkin pie.

"Grace, which one of these knives is for bread?" Jarrett asks.

"That one," she says, pointing to the long serrated one with the wooden handle.

"Which one is for tomatoes?"

"The one with the bigger waves and wider blade."

"If you had to cut up celery, which one would you pick?"

"Trick question. I would use the Cuisinart," she says dramatically, punching the air with her finger.

"Just humor me, Grace. Like there was no electricity, or you were living in Little House on the Prairie or something. Think about the texture of celery. What knife? Would you use the same one as the tomatoes?"

"No. The notches would catch on all those stringy things. I would probably pick a smooth blade. And because it's a hard vegetable, a thicker, heavier one."

He approves of her answer with a slight bow, and she curtsies with the edges of her striped apron.

I close my eyes and take in the scene through my other senses. My heart is calm. Guitar and hand drums come from the living room. Kyle and Chris are running through an acoustic cover of U2's "In the Name of Love."

Our neighbor Kay has popped over for tea, and she's folding napkins for the feast; I overhear her telling sweetly pregnant Sam about her own experience of motherhood. In the morning, a few more assorted travelers will arrive, including my stepmother, my husband's ex-wife and her sister, a newly divorced daddy, a poet who is far from home.

I say a small prayer that all will feel welcomed and loved, embraced and accepted when they come to our door. Nourished in body and soul. We will also hold the memories of our beloved dead, and the promise of new life in our circle.

My eyes open as my husband takes the small of my back and says, "Hello." He whispers in my ear, "It's beautiful, isn't it?" He nods toward the living room, where eighteen-year-old Connor is sprawled on the couch with the old cat as a belly warmer; Connor's leggy girlfriend-of-the-month is at his feet tucked up in ball, sleeping.

"Yes. Yes it is," I say.

This man, who holds this space with his quiet, sexy dignity, with his strong arms and goofy smile—we go forehead to forehead, eyes wide open, and breathe deeply. The boys making music in the other room segue into Ziggy Marley's "Love is My Religion."

That was the Thanksgiving before stage-four throat cancer took John into the depths of himself, into the isolation ward, into radiation and chemotherapy. That was before he spent long afternoons staring silently out the bedroom window, unable to speak. Before his miraculous recovery. Before he ran away into the woods again. Before the post-cancer affairs. Before our divorce.

Cancer:
the Cliff Notes version

AFTER IGNORING A persistent sore throat for almost two years ,
John finally went to the doctor, and then in rapid succession, to an
ENT specialist, who stuck a scope down his throat and said, "Well, you
have a sore throat because there's a tumor blocking 70% of your airway."
We stepped onto a treadmill of diagnostics and waiting rooms and
prognoses. We tried five different doctors, invasive and non-invasive tests.
John was given this diagnosis: Advanced cancer. Stage 4. The potential to
die quickly, or to live a compromised life without a larynx: no speaking,
no swimming, no smelling. The possibility of a long and painful treatment
phase, followed by rehabilitation and skill building. We tried to meet these
possibilities with humor and practicality: We'll learn sign language! There
will be a new way to express ourselves that doesn't involve the voice! When
John got the diagnosis, they gave him a 1 in 10 chance of living out the year.
For all of us, there was a palpable sense of time stopping, of living beneath a
veil. Every interaction was cast in high relief. First, the questions: What does
it mean for our family? How do we treat it? What's the spiritual response?
What's the allopathic medical response? How will we pay for treatment? How
will we pay for our life?

The oncologist's recommendation to John was chemotherapy, "It's going
to kick your ass for a few months, but we're aiming for organ preservation,
so it's worth it." He was optimistic about the treatment, to be followed by
radiation.

This was our season of being still as much as possible. Our season of being
mindful and aware. In the 'busy' season we had missed each other, we had

misunderstood, but there wasn't room for that now. For many months John spent much of his time sitting silently, as he couldn't speak. He stared out the big glass window at the hills, a forced vipassana meditation. The world's demands were still high, but we were changed. This was a time that tested our stability and our steadiness. Usually, we succeeded.

While it was John's cancer, and his direct experience of it all in his body— at the same time, it was *our* cancer because of the prominent role he held in our world, in our tribe. There were many days when I, unkempt and unwashed, dropped him at Dr. Brett's, got him settled in the chair, and ran from the oncology center. I'd close the door on the office and run to the car, singing an anxious little ditty to myself: *I can do this. I can do this. Today I will get my work done. I'm not the one getting chemo; I'm not the one getting chemo. Thank god for this healthy body. Thank god for my healthy body.*

When the treatments were over, John was told to take four weeks of old-fashioned recovery. He was advised to focus on rebuilding his strength and physical integrity, and on preparing to reenter the flow of the world—in whatever way this process had changed him, with whatever new perspectives he'd been given. We had thought he would die, or at the very least lose his ability to speak for the remainder of his life. To our great joy, and everyone's surprise, John was given a clean bill of health.

He spent the next month at the Esalen Institute on the California Coast gardening and eating beautiful food and reimagining his life. Two and a half months later he said he didn't want to be married anymore.

In many families that experience cancer together and survive, there is increased appreciation for each other, a settling into love. But that wasn't our situation. John said he simply couldn't go back to his old life. He didn't want to be a father, he didn't want to be a husband, he didn't want to work like he had worked before. He didn't want to work on it. He wanted to heal, he wanted to live in the woods, he wanted to be a monk. There was no therapy or conversation. In the end, he ended up with a young woman he met during that time at Esalen. You just never know how things will unfold.

Reaction and wisdom do their dance

HOW COULD YOU *do this to me?* I thought. *I got you through cancer, and this is my payback? Was any of what we had real? Or was it all just a con? How could you abandon me?* Along with that, I had all of the anger that came with those questions.

In the same breath as the anger, however, there was a realization that I couldn't really judge him. Even though it wasn't in this context, I had done the same things in my lifetime. I'd been the other woman, allowing a relationship with a married man to develop into shared adventures. I had participated equally with John in the explorations of other models of relationship and sexual expression in our ten years together.

I could *conceptually* understand that for the other woman, this wasn't about *me*; I was likely a non-issue. The connection she was developing with him existed in a vacuum of our family, and had its own soul's purpose. Furthermore I saw that what was happening between John and his array of outside love interests, may have been part of my own karmic reconciliation. In many ways, we were the same. I was him. It reminded me of the spiritual axiom that what we hate most in the other is what we despise in ourselves.

I also had to come to grips with how much the loss of John felt like the abandonment by and loss of my mother—that the depth and pain of my reaction was the screaming memories of an eight year old, getting triggered and projected onto what was happening between two grown up people in choice.

There was another voice speaking, a wisdom voice, one that was centered and clear: I have to honor others' truths, their desires, their unique paths as fully as my own. It is a fundamental form of respect. As I discovered with

John, love will go where it wants to go. It can't be regulated or legislated, and any and all agreements, spoken and unspoken, are subject to change—if not in external form, then in their internal reality. On the outside, you can be married for fifty years and still love someone else. On the outside, you can hold hands with your beautiful husband on the trail and love him with all your heart, while inside still knowing that you have work to do on yourself that will take you far away for a while, and have a poignant sadness inside, knowing both of these things to be true. And so can he.

What's real?

HOW DO YOU make sense of love, especially love coupled with crazy? How do you make sense of longing when it's accompanied by so many fractures and injuries?

John is a writer, like me. The year we married he started writing a book called *Animal Trader* about a man who runs off into the woods and barters with the animals. The opening line is, "We throw it all away or the currents of the highway blow it to the margins." Yes, we throw it all away.

The first chapter is a set-up for how one might disappear into the woods, should one desire to escape life. "But doesn't everyone leave a paper trail? Toilet paper, shredded printer paper, receipts, electronic bread crumbs? If there is a missing persons alert, sooner or later Hertz might get the word. Do they do that? Do Interpol and the FBI alert rental car companies? Whatever. There is no perfect crime, including your own disappearance." He wrote, "Find a trailhead, fill out a backcountry pass, hustle along the trail for a couple of miles—*Just day-hiking, thanks!*—and hit it cross-country."

Maybe he was writing what his heart couldn't say out loud. And while organizing his office and taking pictures and working in the garden and having amazing sex and kicking it in the martial arts studio, he was also getting high every morning. *How could he blow it all up?*

The part of us that decided to be "love fairies," to give and inspire and be present for the community, lived side-by-side with the part of us that was in denial about serious problems with truth telling, especially to each other.

There were so many half-truths in those days I can't even pick them apart. But the most important one of all was his interior untruth: the inability to name what he really wanted. And what is a half-truth anyway, but a lie, another form of disconnection?

Which brings me to a fundamental question: Why do we lie or hide in intimate partnerships, and what can we do about it?

Reimagining intimacy: Telling the truth to one another

> I love my brothers and am bewildered at the nature, and cause, of our alienation from the simple pleasures of presence and connection with our women and children and friends... How could that ever not be enough?
>
> – COLIN SHEPARD COOK

IF I WASN'T fully aligned with the idea that we can redesign our lives and relationships before John's cancer, I certainly moved closer to alignment afterwards. A life or death crisis creates a special dispensation; in this case, allowing a choice that I might not otherwise have been able to make.

It's very compelling to be so connected and present with another human being, to make a family and a home and have all the beauty that entails. But in order for that to last, both people in the relationship need to be honest and transparent about what they need and what they want and be able to tell that to their partner.

So why don't we?

For many of us, feeling exposed, even to the people to whom we are closest, is very uncomfortable if we don't love what is inside ourselves. If we can't love our own dark sides, shadows or broken places, we will never allow others to see them—and we won't be able to love others in theirs, either. Even if we aren't forthcoming about those shadow sides, our partners will probably intuit what they are, maybe even calling us out on them. And when they name the things we cannot accept in ourselves, it's all too easy to become resentful.

When we are in the "hide the suffering" or the lying camp, we have to wear masks. Eventually, that masking creates a gap so wide that any bond with another becomes highly breakable. Wouldn't it be easier if we were able to tell the truth about our inner lives, to help each other get clear on the values that drive each us? It's not our masks people want; it's authenticity.

A great relationship will create a climate that invites this level of dialogue and self-revelation.

People learn over a lifetime to hide their truths. Voicing our shadows and our complexities may be met with anger, scorn, withdrawal or other forms of punishment. So we learn to hold back on discussing those aspects of ourselves, even with our most intimate partners. When we reinforce shame, we reinforce the hiding habit. When our friends share themselves with us, we must accept their truth and not argue, bargain, wheedle, cajole, shame, or punish them.

Just think of what happens when a friend tells us a tiny slice of his reality that isn't so appealing, and we react unfavorably. Their tender shoot of truth telling is squashed.

Our inability to hear other's truths generally stems from our own expectations. Holding people up to our expectations is a recipe for disaster; it produces only disappointment and bitterness. In my case, I wanted John to be steady and stable, and when he wasn't I felt scorn rise up in me. I wanted my kids to have an intact family; when it didn't happen I was bitter and resented other families that seemed to have that. It was my attachment to my desires that were at the root of this suffering, not the situation itself.

I have to believe, and I mean truly believe, *that everybody is doing the best that they can at any given moment.* Given their unique set of experiences, skills, awareness of their own choice and impact, they are always making the best choice in the moment—by virtue of the fact that that is the choice they are making. Even if these choices don't appear to be "good" ones, I can have compassion and understanding; when someone makes a destructive choices, it indicates that he or she is still informed by old pain. And hopefully one day, when the person has done the work, she'll be able to make a different choice.

Of course, improvement and growth is still possible, and the best couples are always growing. There is never a case when someone's whole being is evil or unworthy of love. When I stop faulting people for the things they cannot do, spaciousness opens up in the relationship, and in my heart.

An honest, transparent relationship feels good in the body. It feels clear and somehow safer when people tell the truth about themselves, even if its not easy to hear. It's our job to learn to let others tell their truths without reacting. To let them have their experience even if we wish it to be different.

When two people can talk about their differences and allow compromise to transform them into something else, it's miraculous. We learn to love what is.

Here's another revelation: We can love people where they are, *even if we don't agree with their behavior*. After all, we react to the same circumstances in different ways; behaviors can have multiple meanings to different people. What if we didn't project meaning? What if we just love our partner anyway? How about that?

Loving someone and accepting him or her, however, does not mean you have to be a victim. You can still move out of harm's reach. If the behavior is truly egregious, eventually you can learn to say, "I see that you lie and you cheat, and I can have compassion for the things that make you do that, but it's really poor behavior and it makes me uncomfortable. So I am going to avoid situations in which I can be impacted by that lying and cheating. But I won't close my heart." If I close my heart because someone doesn't behave in the way I expect, or desire, in the way that I think they should, then it hurts me, as well. I create my own suffering.

These days I try to let people be where they are and avoid arguing with their stated needs, even those needs are baffling. I try to say something to the effect of, "I can love you. I don't have to be attached to your life on a daily basis, but I can see you for who you are and love you right there. I don't have to be your closest (friend/wife/lover/business partner/stepmom), but I can love you anyway." That, after all, is how *I* long to be treated.

If we love people, we love them all the time. That's because we accept all of them—even the parts we don't like. We allow our love to be a steady shining sun. We're human, so the light can be occluded temporarily, but the goal is to have it burn steady and wish the other person well.

We can't make another person do what we want or expect. We can never know another's mind fully—character, fears, life arc. And so, out of respect for that person's self-knowledge, *even if we want something different*, we love them anyway. If someone is not showing up in a way that feels good to me, I let that person be where he is and move on, without taking it personally. This narrative around *choosing to love others where they are* flies in the face of the grasping, needy relating that I used to do—and it is awesome.

Transformation instead of abandonment

ANOTHER BIG DISCOVERY: There are no "rules". We can invent any form of relationship we wish. We are adults. We get to choose.

Imagine how much suffering would be reduced if we collectively could transform the current break-up narrative of the culture to another story—one asserting that, even if our romantic connection changes, we can move into a new form of relationship. I've found that people who end relationships often can't stay friends. They may even become bitter and resentful that their expectations of what should have been haven't materialized. The nature of wounds is that sometimes we begin to identify with them, to make the hurt part of who we are. That is a prison of our own making. An ending can be a transformation, instead of a loss.

In contrast, if we don't define ourselves by our own disappointment, and allow people to move on gracefully, wholeness is possible. We might say something like, "a marriage of ten years isn't a failed marriage; it was good until it no longer served us."

There are infinite creative solutions and ways of being together. I know many families who successfully have old and new partners, children from both families at the dinner table, and arrangements ranging from shared child-rearing to shared vacation homes with their former partners. Sometimes the intimacy is also real—they become deep friends (without benefits). The opposite is also in evidence: The dad who refuses to support his kids to spite his wife; the ex-partner who belittles and shames her prior love.

How do these two opposite ends of the spectrum emerge? Often, people haven't been able to sit in their discomfort long enough to navigate to a graceful resolution. This avoidance could stem from a lack of communication skills, a lack of courage to stay in the conversation, an unwillingness to do the deep internal work to not be identified with the outcome of the relationship—or any combination of these things.

People sometimes want the immediate and easy way out: a quick move to the next thing. This behavior leaves a trail of tears, a lifetime of abandoned ties and lost opportunities. It reinforces the notion that people are temporary and life is filled with transactional encounters. Sometimes it's stubbornness: a holding on to hurt or self righteousness, usually driven by one's own shadow self. And almost without fail, nothing is learned, the patterns are repeated, and the cycle goes on.

In shifting a relationship into a new form, one thing that helps is to consciously hold onto the positive connections and memories we experienced together. Any partnership is a combination of good and loving *and* hurtful and sad. Keep the good stuff, too. On the other hand, remembering things as all rosy leads to Maudlin pathos. Try to look at the whole of things. Don't choose the sour taste as the only memory, the black and white: there are many shades of gray.

It may be too hard in the beginning to stay in close connection with your ex, but over time, the practice of blessing the other, wishing the best for them, investigating and learning from our experiences, and working on ourselves may bear very rich fruit.

Redesigning the form

B UT WHAT IF you don't want an ending at all? Or what if you're just setting out and discerning your own path? Sometimes people can't find a rhythm or satisfaction in a traditional monogamous long-term relationship. They become secretive or dissatisfied. But what if, just what IF, we decided to take a more expansive view, and to redesign our intimate relationship to fit our unique situations, our values, and those of the people we love?

Living on the west coast, the hub of lifestyle innovations, I've seen many "alternative" romantic scenarios arise: open relationship, polyamory, serial monogamy, sexual opt-outs. People are documenting and describing these publicly, navigating the new world of ethics and practicalities inherent in these situations.

We can design whatever we'd like, together. We each get to choose—and other people get to choose, too. We get to make a new form of relationship that doesn't play on old tropes. What will we make together, if we choose to be in growth?

Letting Love Grow Again

Everybody has a hungry heart.
Everybody needs a place to rest.
Everybody wants to have a home.
Don't make no difference what nobody says.
Ain't nobody want to be alone.

— BRUCE SPRINGSTEEN

It would have been an easy to shut down desire, or curtail my willingness to open up again fully to someone after John. But instead, I was intent on using this as a healing crisis, and growing stronger and more open. My friend Adam (a yogi, musician, and relationship educator), really helped me in this process. Adam lives the communication skills he's spent so many years learning: he taught me how to respond in real time when a small sting came up or an annoyance arose between people. He modeled for me the incredible power of staying in a difficult conversation, without running or hiding. The power of staying kind and present in the face of changing relationships. With him, I practiced how to hold my own center to be able to really listen to another, how to speak without blaming. How to take myself lightly.

In addition to Adam, I sought out as much knowledge as I could. I put in the time and attention to learn as much as I could about communication, non violent communication, unconditional love, the languages of love, and self-mastery so that if I did enter into a new relationship, I would be better resourced when a difficult subject or moment arose.

So there I was, living up on the mountain overlooking San Francisco Bay, wanting to keep choosing love.

Yet, at that time, even with a big family and many friends, I felt isolated. Let me rephrase that: *I was choosing isolation.* I still felt awkward with our couple friends, often like a third wheel. I didn't want to burden people with my story or the shadow of what had just happened, nor send a signal to my single (or married, for that matter) guy friends that would invite misunderstanding.

I didn't know what form I wanted love to take, what I wanted or desired, or what I was capable of showing up for. I wanted to keep some of this newly discovered freedom to run my own day: I wanted more space to write and train, less intertwining of money and laundry, along with the juicy good parts of intimate connection: the long arc of friendship, having each other's back, great sex, growing and traveling together, shared purpose and meaning.

The only thing to do was to put on my big girls pants and make some effort to meet new people. So, I started in the lowest commitment way possible: on Craigslist and Tinder, as authentically as I could but with low expectations. Like anything else, I dove in. 15 dates in 2 weeks. 5 second dates. 3 third dates. Out of that, 2 new friends and one great romance.

First discovery: there are so many cool people out there, doing so many interesting things. Second discovery: There won't always be a fit, and that's okay; I made some friends anyway. It's not about anyone's absolute value (not mine or theirs)—it's about the match. With some people, I felt easy and funny and beautiful, and with some people like a messy, mute gorilla. Within minutes it was apparent if there was an energy match. The "energy" being indicated by whether the sense of humor and values seemed to connect, and if there was a physical spark. If there wasn't a match, I just tried to learn as much as I could about their world, needs and expertise—could I help? Third discovery: there is an abundance of rich possibilities for loving—everybody really *does* have a hungry heart.

One night, I wanted to go to hear some live music at this little jewel of a theater in town, and saw a guy's notice in the online "just friends" postings. He'd put "you'll probably bore me" in the title, which made me laugh and wonder what he was so confident about. He littered his notes with subtle literary references. We emailed a bunch, and talked, and his voice on the phone made my belly flutter.

Finally, we decided to meet for dinner. Before we set the time and date, he said, "I have to tell you something. I'm a very large person, almost seven feet tall. It can startle people on first meeting."

I asked in return, "Has that been a problem with women in the past?"

There was a long pause. "Never with the right women."

I said, "Well, I shaved my head two months ago as a post divorce cleansing gesture, so while I'm not quite in full Sinead mode, that may also be startling."

And we left it at that.

We met at little family Italian place on the town square. He felt like an old friend on first glance; a great warmth suffused me on seeing his dancing eyes and strong Viking ship-captain face. That dinner lasted hours. The conversation lasted hours. And so it began.

Music, and hiking, and dinners in and out, writing together, exploring. He rowed crew in college, and was a physically powerful man, a filmmaker, writer and producer who later in life became a technophile. We took it easy and slow.

A few months in, he called me with an unusually serious tone in his voice.

"So," he said, "you might be wondering why I haven't made a move on you. I want you to know that I'm crazy attracted to you and want to love you up and down, but I'm nervous."

"Why? Is there a problem?"

"No, but I haven't been with anyone in three years, since I split with my ex, and I'm worried I'll do it wrong."

"Umm... does everything work alright?"

He laughed. "Yes. Yes, it does."

"Well, cool, then we have an opportunity. I haven't been with anyone either. Let's both get tested, and then, if we do decide to have sex, you know.... we can have a fluid relationship from the beginning."

And we did just that, like teenagers. We went to Planned Parenthood separately, and texted each other the results. Eventually he carried me across the threshold of a little inn on the coast, and the nature of our friendship shifted to a juicy and passionate love affair.

There have been so many beautiful moments: Easter in the Khalil Gibran gardens in Washington DC, sea kayaking on the coast, drinking whiskey in the dark on the beach. The most profound times, though, have been random mornings or weeknights of intimacy. Making the coffee, doing morning gratitudes and intentions, or something equally mundane. One night, in an absolute deluge, rain and wind pummeling the house, bending trees, we lay down on the sheepskin rug, bundled in flannel and wool, flat on our backs, and played 'spin the Spotify' wheel, handing the controls back and forth: *Have you heard this? 'Member this?*

That night, we let the waterfall of sound and story run through our ears and down down down our bodies. We listened to *Skinny Love*, Bon Iver's original AND Birdy's cover, which transforms it into a different thing altogether. We listened to the tender optimism that is Griffin House and the Wood Brothers. He picked a song to share, because, he says, "of a specific moment when Emmylou comes up under Willie; that one suspended note is the heart of the song". The song started to play: Willie and Emmylou and Daniel Lanois singing "The Maker." He grasped my hand to his chest, hugged it tight, closed his eyes, and whispered, "Here it comes…here it comes, do you hear it? That harmony? That way of joining?" My ears went out to meet the music, to hear what he heard in this reverie. In this easy love on a work night, at home, I felt that sheer merciful relief of being home again, of never-not-home— what to me is the most wonderful feeling in the world.

For several years, we waxed and waned. There were complicating anxieties and his difficult ex, but we seem to always come back. There was learning. We did some great work together with relationship educators Don and Martha Rosenthal, 40 years married, radiant people. Don and Martha teach 'Awakening Together: relationship as a spiritual practice'. Difficult moments became less frequent, and as the years passed and we traversed each other's successes and failures and growth edges and potholes, we came to love each other deeply. We never co-habited, although we talked about land near the Oregon border; he wanted an acre with a well and a pasture. We didn't co-parent his school-aged daughter, although she is an absolute love. He's prone to isolation, he goes deep into his workshop, making things like Arduino computers and fussing around with his 3D printer, or solving some technical glitch in a software he's written; there might not be a peep for days. Still, we fundamentally had each other's back, day to day and week to week—when someone was in the hospital or vendors didn't pay their bills on time, or the Christmas lights needed to come down or the garden wanted planting, or a good scream/cry/laugh was needed. All my life, I've had a tendency to "want what I want when I want it." So this longer unfolding has been teaching me patience, the value of the slow reveal.

We've chosen friendship, not romance, now. There have been other inquiries along the way, a truth-challenged Irish Catholic tri-athlete and investment banker; a poignant and profound connection with someone who was already bound and committed to another; an older adventuring man—all with their own beauties.

Now, I'm inviting in a relationship with spirit at the center, a rich alliance based on kindness and growth, with one or more people. It's a pretty good place to be landing.

In moving toward a new kind of being in relationship, here are the things I've found useful. First, I've been practicing really knowing what is right for me. I've learned to recognize what is a full yes and a full no—and when the yes is coming from pleasing or compliance, and when the no is coming from fear. One of the challenges of getting 'wired to please' early in life is you have to keep working conscientiously, to deeply pay attention to what you really feel.

I've been practicing a compassion for people, just letting them be them-selves—trying to be more interested in what's real for them than in how their choices or thoughts impact me. I'm trying not to project or make my own meaning out of their actions, but to stay in open communication, and be in the moment. "I will let you be where you are. I will love you where you are. I will manage my own stuff and won't expect anything, and let's see what unfolds."

Maybe the most important practice is this one: the "managing my own stuff" piece. To me, this means that there's no more wanting to be rescued. I take responsibility for my work and health and money and housing. I take responsibility for my own happiness. It's no one else's job to make any of that stuff happen for me. There's no Prince Charming. That removes any kind of transactional element from the romantic story. I let go of the way I want it to be, and instead love the way it is, or leave the situation.

This flavor of romance is infinitely more beautiful, and completely different than the limited, transactional one I'd previously imagined.

Profoundest love

HAVE YOU HAD the experience of suddenly perceiving everything at once, of all things working in harmony and ease? How amazing and miraculous it all is?

Once, driving down the highway in the Sonoma springtime, I had a sudden awareness of everything growing around me—all of nature, with no help or planning or control, working together of a piece, a perfect system that required no toil or effort. It just was. And I wasn't separate from that system. I pulled over to the side of the road, and let my awareness stay in a temporary bird's eye perception of the hills and countryside, the bay and the mountains, all deeply interconnected. When the awareness passed, I turned on the car and continued driving home.

Later, I would learn from my friend Bernie, a pioneer in soundscapes, that ecosystems govern themselves through sound. If a species moves out, the species that moves in sounds at the same pitch and at the same time of day as the species that left. The natural world self-regulates through harmonics—species are always communicating their presence. So it is in the world of bacteria and viruses—they are continually sending signals to one another, both to coordinate actions and to regulate the distance between themselves. Mushrooms convey signals to one another, as well as on behalf of other plants; Mycelium networks form a sort of telecommunication system in the soil. There is an invisible network present between humans also, what my friend Reese Jones calls the limbic internet—a group awareness and emotional governance that requires no verbal communication. In other words: Connectivity and networks are the fundamental design and nature of all things.

That day driving in Sonoma wasn't the only time this kind of supra-perception has happened for me. Once, up on the coast, I had the distinct sense perception of everything merging: my own molecules indistinguishable from what was around me. I was the water, I was the mist above the water, I was the sand, I was the space between the sand and the water.

Over the years, there have been other moments of seeing reality differently. I remember one time walking into a conference room where very sophisticated, powerful people sat around the table, and having a fleeting perception of all the gathered as seven-year olds, with children's faces, just trying to figure the world out. It hit me in a flash: *We are all our ages at one time.*

Or this: The night my father died, I was too far away to be with him in person, so I went into a deep meditation and talked with him for a long while. Near the end of the conversation, I told him, "You were a great father, you can go now, release the pain. Thank you, I love you, please forgive me, I forgive you. " I came out from the meditation, only to stare at the walls in the roadside Best Western until morning. My son, who'd arrived days before to my father's house, called at sunrise, and reported that the evening prior, my dad had been in an agitated state, saying my name a lot, and that he had fallen into a coma, coincidentally, I discovered, at the exact moment I came out of that meditation. He died in the night.

These glimpses of what is really going on at the tiniest level, and the systems level, are both bewildering, and somehow have created deep moments of peace. To know that I am connected to all of life, to all beings, at the cellular level, and that we are all acting on each other all the time is exciting, it has so much potential.

There's a little book called *"After Enlightenment, the Laundry."* I'm not saying I'm enlightened, what I'm saying is that these mystical experiences are always followed by dropping back into the more common reality. Taking the sense of the unity experienced in those moments back into my ordinary life takes actual practice and skills. To remember unity when the bills are piling up, to remember unity when someone's cheated you, to remember unity when the political sphere is filled with ugliness. To live from profound love, to live with an attitude of truly seeing the other's divinity, to live with an internalized love of life and all beings, to seek unity and similarity over division, to join with the other first.

Some people think this 'connective' attitude is soft, that it's an easy way to live, but it can actually be quite challenging.

The easy thing is to fight. To insist. To overpower the other. The harder path is understanding. To be able to practice profound love isn't a soft or optional skill—it's a necessity for evolving our lives together in a civil society. .

Idealism Shaming

WHAT I CALL "Idealism Shaming" is a real thing. It's a phenomenon in which those who think of themselves as realists (or rational, or practical, or analytical) criticize or belittle those who espouse a world vision in which greater peace, justice, love and understanding dominate. While we celebrate King or Gandhi or Mandela or Malala or Suu Kyi, they are treated as exceptions for their bravery, while many 'everyday idealists' are dismissed as naive, new age, lightweight, utopian, pollyanna, or just plain unintelligent—especially by those with a combative worldview or those who are invested in conflict.

I've been working in technology for decades. It's getting more and more powerful, accelerating in capacity and independence. Machine vision, emotion recognition, artificial intelligence, robotics, genomics—wow, it is all happening so fast. Right now the technology goes both ways for us as a species—it helps us cure rare diseases and generate energy in new ways, while at the same time it's damaging the oceans and enabling mass murderers. In other words, our tools have no moral compass. They will be used to serve and amplify the spiritual state of humankind—in Brussels or Lahore, New York or San Jose. The more powerful our technologies and tools become, the greater the urgency for us to have concurrent spiritual development.

We have never before seen so clearly and immediately the impact of our divisions; the incredible suffering that fear, posturing, othering, labeling, and hate produce in the world. We're going to need a lot of psycho-social-emotional skills to meet these divisions with our eyes wide open and counteract them. We will need profound love and wisdom. A lot of spiritual bravery,

AND every possible voice to be an instrument in improvising and navigating a collective shift away from anger, separation and violence toward profound interconnection.

People often talk about artists being the most sensitive and vigilant members of society; I believe that they are the harbingers of what's wrong within our culture. They see it and sense it and pick it up before others do. They are the canaries in the coalmine of our cultural brokenness. I enjoy seeking them out and hearing what they say. For example, one of the artists I know personally was dealing with questions such as *how shall we power human societies on earth*—far before the dialogue on peak oil came into public dialogue. Another is dealing with the *psychological impacts of being "walled in" or "walled out" on the US-Mexico border.* Another's art investigates the *fatigue of the working family*—issues that were on her radar before they entered political conversation. Even those others might consider "crazy", more often than not, have a kernel of truth to offer.

We NEED the sensitives, the artists, the idealists now more than ever.

You know that part of you that is seven, or eight or nine? The part that loves belonging, acceptance, play, creation, joy, making, figuring things out, connection, joining, investigating—the part that knows wonder first hand? When that part is coming up, please let it come! Want it. Name it. Desire it. For yourself. For your friends and kids and neighbors. For everyone. Don't be cool.

If the self-proclaimed realists of this world want to label you a fool, you can name it. Call their response what it is: Idealism Shaming. Then go on and be a brilliant fool in the service of this planet and all of humankind, for a better way of living together. You are the instrument. I am the instrument. We are the instruments.

CONCLUSION

Beginning again

WHETHER IT'S VIOLENCE, illness, poverty or lost love, this thing called living presents us a lot of opportunities to give up. Some people walk away, drop out, freeze, settle, get bitter, turn to drugs, or get overpowered by any number of systems. Why are there those who are almost organically short-circuited by trauma, deadened in some way? Conversely, why are others able to lay new wires, build new circuits, dig deeper, and transform as a result of what happens to them? Why are some people zealously able to focus on their mission in the face of all kinds of subtle and overt repressive efforts whether as minor as social disapproval or as major as imprisonment, harassment or physical threat, while others buckle?

I've been thinking a lot about resilience. A long arc of a lifetime of achievement requires resilience and tenacity. It may be someone known, like the esteemed biologist E.O. Wilson who, after a lifetime of scientific leadership, has just published his first novel. Or it may be an unknown, like the Sansomes—a beautiful couple in their 80s who run a sustainable Christmas Tree Farm together in California's High Sierra, rising each day to restore the forests with baby Sequoias.

How do they do it? Is the difference in character, genetics, beliefs, experiences? A combination of those? Something else? Is it resilience, or its more conscious relative, courage? Or some combination of the two, that makes one thrive where the other falls away? And what if we each began to look at each experience a chance to say not "This sucks," but "Wow, what happens next?"

I used to think that the traumatic things that happened to us in life were a curse, but I was wrong. Now I see these experiences as preparing me to serve. At some point we have to do our own forgiveness work around bad memories. Even if they are horrifying and ugly, there is still something in our worst memories that can bless our lives. A bad experience can be a point of departure from which we bring service to others. It can prepare us for some new beginning, some new perspective. In order to accommodate ourselves with the world at large, there has got to be a reconciliation. All the things that happen to us may have, as part of their fruit, some opportunity or blessing.

One key element of resilience is reconciliation with things that have happened, and with people. A return to wholeness. Reconciliation can happen very simply, without any change on anyone else's part. It can happen with parents: If we simply say, "I see you. I see what you did to bring me into the world. I see the long chain of suffering that preceded you bringing me into the world, all my grandmothers and great grandmothers. I can see that even if nothing else happens, even if you left me the day that I was born, even if you were mean to me, you gave me breath and body and I appreciate that effort. I will take it from here. I've got enough."

It can happen with our religion of origin. It can happen with circumstances that occurred that were out of our control—natural disasters or loss. The point is that these past experiences can't be changed, and the ongoing harboring of resentment or ill will only impairs forward progress. It anchors us in negativity.

Throughout life, I have found myself in edgy situations. Initially they found me, but then I started seeking them out because they are so instructive. I have become more conscious of edges, and of the extremes and the clarity they bring. The most extreme experiences, good and bad, have shown me that we are sometimes led into the places that we need to be. There is synchronicity, and a kind of divine guidance, around many corners. Whether it's prison or cancer or the cannabis economy or stepping into a radical church, going to the edges creates a new center. The edge teaches us about the middle, our "normal" daily life. Positive or negative, extremes help us learn how to act and react with poise. I have learned that by practicing being brave (acting even when fear is present), and embracing these explorations, I can actively build the resilience muscle.

Eye gazing with Indra

Far away in the heavenly abode of the great god Indra, there is a wonderful net which has been hung by some cunning artificer in such a manner that it stretches out infinitely in all directions. In accordance with the extravagant tastes of deities, the artificer has hung a single glittering jewel in each "eye" of the net, and since the net itself is infinite in dimension, the jewels are infinite in number. There hang the jewels, glittering like stars in the first magnitude, a wonderful sight to behold.

If we now arbitrarily select one of these jewels for inspection and look closely at it, we will discover that in its polished surface there are reflected all the other jewels in the net, infinite in number. Not only that, but each of the jewels reflected in this one jewel is also reflecting all the other jewels, so that there is an infinite reflecting process occurring.
— FRANCIS HAROLD COOK, ON Indra's net.

NOT LONG AGO, I found myself on a night excursion to Mount Tamalpais, for the monthly gathering of stargazers. After a 45-minute talk on comets and meteors, held in a natural amphitheater, the astronomer turned off all of the lights. It was a new moon, and a dark sky. About a hundred people were lying on their backs looking up at the vastness. The astronomer took out a giant laser pointer. She traced the planets, the stars and the visible constellations. *Here's where our planet is situated right now. This is where you live.*

Afterwards, a group of amateur astronomers who had brought telescopes set them up in the parking lot. We wandered from scope to scope, wearing red headlamps so we wouldn't disturb the light. A passionate community of amateur astronomers and stargazers lived right here; an entire world of people who I did not know existed before this night.

Time and time again I'm reminded of the richness of community, the unknowable diversity that lives among us. The simple act of stargazing with strangers told me this again: Both human communities and the natural world *show* and *know* that we are never alone, never isolated fragments, but always part of the interconnected fabric of all existence.

That connection is profoundly present in intimacy. Have you ever done eye gazing with a friend or lover? You stare into each other's eyes, soften your gaze, and, all of a sudden, the other person disappears. You are looking directly into a person's pupils, and what you see within them, beyond them, is a galaxy. You see the entire universe. And your eyes are reflected back in theirs: Indra's net.

It takes effort to practice this kind of connection on a daily basis. But by creating the containers to create and experience connection, our awareness of this connection becomes more present and steady. We choose connection. And in the choice and action, it drops a pebble. The ripples fan out—from self to family to strangers to community to institution, and back again. Humans have gathered forever, but in our age of separate dwellings, and in our busy-ness, it can take more effort.

When my living room is full of people, gathering, laughing, dining and playing together, I see it as a profound sanctuary. Month after month, year after year, it steals my heart. It's all here: all that is sacred. The great goodness of all life, the breath that breathes all this into possibility, are right here in this room.

We have tools for living in connection. We have tools for treating ourselves and others nonviolently—*not* injuring, *not* harming. If I am suffering or sad, I know the tools that work for me. My personal prescription is a combination of doing something nice for someone else, breathing, gratitude practice, dancing, or most profoundly, going to the yoga mat. It works every time, and I am still surprised that it works.

If we know our own tools and prescriptions for coming back into connection, we can build better families, communities, institutions and systems. We can build new ways of living together: shoulder-to-shoulder, deeply united and lifting others up as part of an infinite, multi-generational family constellation.

We are never separate. We are never alone. Let us be brave together, reconnect, and reweave a culture and a world that works for everyone.

EPILOGUE

St. Christopher's call

M Y FIRST VISIT to San Quentin coincided with John's cancer diagnosis. We were just beginning to understand how severe it was. So, I went home after that first day at San Quentin with the sense that something big had opened up around my mother's death. I lay down next to him on the big bed, and told him what had happened in the prison. We sat there, holding hands, aware that this was going to be a profound and intense time for both of us, and suspecting that we were on very separate healing paths.

My dreams became more vivid than usual around this time. I had nightmares and visitations. One night, in existential fear of losing John, I fell asleep with questions on my mind. Would I ever trust? Would I ever be at home?

There was a beautiful island, white sands and lush grasses and hills and lovely houses with abundant land and space, clean water, ease. I was part of a group of people who shared a feeling of deep friendship and quiet, we had arrived there together. Just after arriving, we felt an anxiety begin to build. Native inhabitants, large and threatening, were doing their ritual dance in the distance. They were chasing us. We had to stay ahead of them.

We moved from one beautiful space to another. In each we generated our own panicky departure—it's time to go, now-now-now—and a futile guardedness of our own invention. Inside of one sun-filled sanctuary, for example, the windows were gracious and wide and open, but the doors had dozens of deadbolts theoretically blocking people from entering— when in reality, all they would have to do is come through the window.

Near the morning, one of our group members emerged from a sunken stone tub and then descended into large white down cushions, announcing, "I would like to stop moving, stop being chased. I would like to rest. I will stay here."

With his declaration, the "enemies" became silent, got into a boat and rowed away. I saw that the "enemies" were only playing our game, only half-heartedly agreeing to chase us.

The message was clear: You are already home. You have what you need. All the running is a game of your own making.

Throughout the dream, there was a shadow figure—a giant man, who I eventually recognized as St. Christopher. Christopher was a Canaanite, more than seven feet tall. He wanted to serve the most powerful king in the world, so he sought him out. Then, one day, when his King was out walking, a passerby said the name of the devil, at which point the King made the sign of the cross. Christopher pressed the king, "Why did you make this sign?," and the King responded "to protect us from the devil."

Christopher said, "Well, if you're afraid of the devil, the devil must be more powerful than you. I will go serve him." But the devil also had fear: when confronted by a woman holding out a cross in self-protection, he cowered.

So Christopher went to discover the power of this cross—what was this thing that stopped the devil in his tracks? He was led to a hermit who told him of the Christ.

"How can I follow this Christ?" St. Christopher asked.

The hermit offered fasting and prayer as a path, which Christopher rejected. The hermit then asked, "Do you know of a river where many perish crossing it?"

"Why, yes," said Christopher.

"You are of fine limb and great power. You will serve well by ferrying people across this river in his name." That's how Christopher became the ferryman, the protector of travelers, the guide from one bank to another. He is reputed to have carried thousands of people to safety, thus earning sainthood.

To me, the moral in the end is that Christopher chose service to all, and he chose the most powerful force of connection we have. Christopher chose love.

CHRISTINE HAS BEEN A LEADER IN THE TECH SECTOR for 20 years, as the venture backed founder and CEO of several companies. She has always been a convener, bringing people together to have conversations around growth and change, and to spark action around new possibilities. She is the curator of 9 TEDxs, the convener of Naked Conversations, founder of LoveSpring, Exquisite, and the Frequency. Her own deep journey exploring anger, violence and disconnection in the aftermath of her mother's murder, early abandonment and general chaos have propelled her explorations into the interior life and capacity of the individual to heal and connect; her work as a victims' right advocate for restorative justice and prison reform; and as an investigator into the neuroscience of human evolution and behavioral change. Christine holds a MBA from the JL Kellogg School of Management at Northwestern University and is a Phi Beta Kappa graduate of Northwestern University in Political Science, with a senior thesis in Arab Nationalism. She served in the US Army ROTC program through the University of Illinois at Champaign-Urbana. She has lived and traveled all over the world, and speaks French and German. She is a yoga teacher and musician. She's mother to 4 of her own children, and co-parent to 2 girls.